TRILLER

a true alternative to TikTok?

The no bullshit perspective for marketers, brands and everybody interested in finding a second short video home!

Markus Rach

Copyright

Dedication

To my rockstar wife Jeanette and my little troublemakers Maximilian & Sophie-Lisanne.

Thank you for letting me do, what I do!

Love you!

Table of Content

Foreword

We live in times of high uncertainty and constant move. At the time of writing this book, the outcome of the 46th presidential election in the US is still not known. Votes are being counted. The Donald is tweeting, and the world is struggling with the global COVID-19 pandemic. Depending on the outcome of the US-elections, amongst other factors, the star of the global short-video market, TikTok, might yet again find itself on wobbly feet, facing a potential US ban. This would leave 100 Million US TikTok users stranded. This would also free up, on average, one hour of these users' time on any given day. Time, most users should probably spend on education or advancing their lives, vs. watching Charli in yet another Dunkin' Donuts commercial. But wait, Charli D'amelio, the most followed creator on TikTok, has already found an alternative platform. So have many other TikTok users.

This alternative is Triller! An app in hypergrowth! An app capitalizing upon the negative press around TikTok and an app ready to provide millions of users a new home in the ever-growing short video market. This book seeks to explore this app and provides insights into world of Triller, its very history, its culture and much more. This book will however also highlight some of the dangers of today's social media world. These dangers do not just apply to Triller, they apply to all digital technology seeking to influence users' behavior. Also, this book aims to entertain! In a world, in which 15 seconds decide upon having millions of followers or a dead account; entertainment is key!

I also need to warn you! I am a marketing & digital technology lecturer in Switzerland and guest lecture in China. Adding to this, I have over 15 years of international marketing experience and run my own consultancy. But, I truly believe that advertising s...cks! Lucky for me, I am not alone with this opinion! Just scan the following QR-Code to hear a well-known NYU-Stern professor speak out on the subject!

Thus, my views and perspectives are not the usual marketing lovefest, celebrating every app as an additional chance to display more advertising to consumers. I try to look with you behind the scenes to understand the interplay of platforms, users and creators. What you make of it, is up to you!

So, let's rock this and explore the world of Triller (through the eyes of a marketing rebel).

How to read this book

Did you know, that in every minute of 2020, 41'666'667 messages are being exchanged on WhatsApp? That 147'000 photos are being uploaded to Facebook? Well, now you do! To give you bragging rights in front of family and friends, check out figure 1 for more crazy statistics!

Figure 1. 1 minute in 2020[1]

---

[1] https://www.socialmediatoday.com/news/what-happens-on-the-internet-every-minute-2020-version-infographic/583340/

And? What's the point of this?

Well, how does one write a book about an app like Triller? A book that aims to be relevant and up to date? Seems almost impossible, right?!

To make the impossible however happen, this book makes use of some of the technology that big tech is throwing at us. Your smartphone! Various blogs, articles, videos and other media are being linked via QR-Codes.

To use these QR-Codes, just grab your smartphone, which is likely in arm's reach! Open the native camera app on your smartphone and focus on the QR-Code. This will trigger a notification to open your browser. I recommend you consume the suggested media along the way, as the content linked will either support my message or provide an alternative perspective.

Let's network!

Since we talk about social media in this book and since it is likely, that you and I have never met, why don't we change this? Hook me up on LinkedIn to exchange further thoughts on Triller, the short video market, or how technology is likely to influence our lives, our behavior and even our attitudes and opinions. This marks also your second QR-Code challenge!

One more thing!

Before we start this book, I need to disclose, that I do run an active TikTok account. As you know, TikTok is the most hyped app in the world of short videos. If you didn't know this, check out chapter 2. Thus, as a marketer and as an academic, I had no choice but to get to know the app firsthand. Hence, I started my own TikTok account in January 2020. I have been active on this account since then and learned a lot. I have learned a lot about the media behavior of generation z, or the difficulty to create engaging 15 second content. Also, I have learned about the very intricacies of an AI-driven platform. This has resulted in my account receiving 4 temporary bans, 4 shadow bans and 1 permanent ban on TikTok. Yep, you heard that right! That makes me the pound for pound baddest academic on the planet! However, I did not mean to get banned. More on this later. Scan the following QR-Code to get to my TikTok account!

Don't worry – you won't see me dancing to the WAP![2]

---

[2] WAP is the name of a 2020 song by Cardi B. The song received wide attention on social media, particularly amongst teenagers. Both its lyrics as well as the song's choreography are rather provocative.

But does this matter for a book about Triller? Well, TikTok and almost every other social media platform, monetizes through advertising. That means, that the app makes money by exposing its user to advertising. The more user it has and the longer these users stay on the app to engage with the app's content, the more monetization opportunities are being generated. Like every other business, a for profit technology company does of course strive to maximize its revenue stream.

So far, so good! Right? But, what if, this company could influence the duration of its users on the app, the engagement of its users with the content and also the creation of relevant content to impact users' engagement? What if this company could also control the ability of brands to reach platform users organically? What if such a company would restrict this organic reach for branded content? Wouldn't that mean, that this company could control its demand, as well as its supply side? Well… we are going to talk about this more in chapter 4, but for now, let me make a very provocative statement:

TikTok is the world's most prominent and most neglected operant conditioning experiment of all time! Not even Facebook can take this title from TikTok!

Thus, the world needs competition in the short video space and Triller marks one competitor with the potential to rise up the ranks to the very top.

Chapter 1: Overview

This chapter introduces Triller as a company, as an app and as the biggest and most notable competitor to TikTok! No offense to others!

The company

Triller was launched in 2015 by David Leiberman[3] and Sammy Rubin[4]. While Leiberman is still with the company, Rubin left Triller in 2017, starting a new venture the following year. Mike Lu[5] became the CEO of Triller in 2017.

Although Triller was originally aimed to be a music video editing tool, using AI to support the stitching of clips, it morphed into a social media platform in 2016. Triller had 4 notable funding rounds since 2015, summing up to USD 37.5 million, as shown in figure 2.

⥮ Announced Date	Transaction Name	Number of Investors	Money Raised
Oct 23, 2019	Series B - Triller	4	$28M
Feb 7, 2018	Series A - Triller	1	$5M
Jun 1, 2015	Seed Round - Triller	1	–
Jun 1, 2015	Seed Round - Triller	1	$4.5M

Figure 2. Triller funding rounds[6]

---

[3] https://www.linkedin.com/in/david-leiberman-3aaa674/

[4] https://www.linkedin.com/in/sammy-rubin-879a7785/

[5] https://www.linkedin.com/in/mikelu07/

[6] https://www.crunchbase.com/organization/triller/company_financials

Throughout these funding rounds, Triller had a total of 7 listed investors. Carnegie Technologies marked the lead investor in the Series A round, while Proxima Media joined as the lead investor in the latest Series B round.

The Series B investment marked an important milestone for Triller, as Proxima Media added financial resources, but also industry expertise to Triller. Bobby Sarnevesht, a partner at Proxima Media, joined Triller, as part of the deal, in the role of executive chairman.[7] This has given the platform more access to an even broader network within the music industry.

Further, Triller has been reported to be preparing for another USD 250 million round of funding, raising its valuation to USD + 1 billion.[8] Unicorn status: check!

---

[7] https://www.prnewswire.com/news-releases/triller-announces-record-breaking-growth-new-funding-by-proxima-media-and-acquisition-of-ai-music-platform-300944115.html

[8] https://techcrunch.com/2020/08/04/triller-tiktok/

Triller's history leads to an important differentiation of Triller to many other short video focused apps. Triller did not define itself as a short video platform, but as an "AI-powered music video app", allowing its users to create professionally looking videos without much effort. Today, its core remains still very much with the very spirit of the founders: to democratize the music video editing process.

On that basis, Triller is often falsely compared to TikTok as just another short video app. Triller offers a fundamentally different experience, although latest updates and the addition of new features spark the Triller-TikTok comparison yet again. More on this in the following section.

There's however one question that still needs to be answered! How does Triller make money?

A recent Business Insider India article shines light on this! Please read the extract below.

"Explaining the revenue model behind Triller, Roohparvar said "Triller makes a profit through brand partnerships, sponsorship, integration deals along with live events and pay-per-view, like the upcoming, highly-anticipated fight between mike Tyson and Roy Jones Jr set for November 28. Another example was this summer's virtual talent contest, the first of its kind, STEP UP to the Mic powered by Boost Mobile, and

which reached more viewers than American Idol and X Factor combined."[9]

There you have it! Smart and value providing content, which draws the attention of different user demographics to Triller. As such, one could assume, that the Mike Tyson comeback gains the attention of a slightly older age group compared to Triller's "STEP UP to the mic" talent show. Again, smart! These partnership and sponsorship deals provide also a great opportunity for brands to reach their target groups in a non-intrusive manner. Whilst Triller is still in a growth phase, brands probably have a chance to secure an early mover "bargain deal".

We will further look into marketing options on Triller in chapter 3.

---

[9] https://www.businessinsider.in/advertising/ad-tech/article/how-triller-app-smartly-poached-top-tiktokers-and-its-cso-to-become-the-no-1-in-app-store-with-zero-marketing-budget/articleshow/77614603.cms

Triller vs. TikTok

Although, as previously mentioned, Triller is often compared to TikTok, both apps differ in fundamental aspects. Some of those, based on the November 2020 state of development of both applications, are detailed below.

Focus on Music

Let's start with the obvious one. Triller grew as an AI driven app to democratize the creation of music videos and it does this very well. Users can not only choose from Triller's vast selection of songs on the app, driven by Triller's growing list of partnerships within the music industry, but also import their own songs, or add songs from Spotify or Apple Music. Further, Triller's extensive agreements with the music industry allow users to listen to the full song, or select the part of the song to which they seek to perform, up to 60 seconds.

Editing Features

This is most notable difference between Triller and TikTok. Whilst TikTok offers extensive in-app editing features, filters and effects, Triller focuses on AI supported editing of music videos. For users transitioning from TikTok to Triller, this feels rather restricting. At least on the very beginning. However, Triller provides the choice to either create a music video, or, as an alternative, a social video. Social videos, which are categorized further into dance, comedy and other genres, provide also extensive user editing features. However, social videos do not allow to include a soundtrack or music.

User vs. Leaderboards

While Triller is an AI based editing platform, TikTok is an AI based user-engagement platform. Meaning, TikTok optimizes itself based on the exhibited behavior of each user to increase the rate of interaction with the app's content, as well as the overall user duration on the app. This is easily notable by visiting TikTok's For You Page (FYP). Through that engagement focus, TikTok has managed to almost match the daily app-usage time of Facebook. On average, users spend 52 minutes per day on TikTok, vs. 58 minutes on Facebook.[10]

Compared to TikTok and its efforts to optimize engagement rates on the app, Triller displays content through the focus on leaderboards, challenges, trends and genres. Although Triller has a feature called Trills to somewhat mirror TikTok's For You Page experience, it does not yet succeed to capture the user in the same addictive way. This is also notable in Triller's reported time users spend per day on the app. As such, Triller users are reported to spend on average 22 minutes per day on the app.[11]

Also, while no user has yet managed to reach the end of TikTok's FYP, scrolling through the Triller Trills is finite, meaning you do seem to reach its end in only a few seconds if you keep scrolling.

Is this necessarily a bad thing? Probably not from the point of view of many parents, educators and psychologists. Prolonged

---

usage times of smartphones and thus apps have been empirically linked to various health conditions, or even developmental dysfunctionalities of minors. However, from the point of view to provide TikTok users a second home, it probably is a bad thing. Thus, to answer the above, one would have to clarify in which category Triller wants to play in the future. Does Triller aim to stick to its roots as a music video editing platform, or does it aim to replicate the social and entertainment nature of the short video app trend found on TikTok? Time will probably tell.

Celebrities

Another notable difference between TikTok and Triller is the focus on star-power. Triller is very actively promoting its star and celebrity power on the platform. Some of the stars frequently using the app are Marshmello, Eminem, Alicia Keys and many others. On top, Triller has gotten quite some attention by promoting the return of Mike Tyson against Jones Jr, which will take place in late 2020. The pre-fight conference was hosted live on Triller, capitalizing upon the event's star power.[12] This event, marked "Tyson on Triller", is yet again pushing Triller away from its home of music video editing, see figure 3. Maybe this has to do with how Triller sees its own positioning in the marketplace. In a CNBC interview, Ryan Kavanaugh revealed that Triller sees itself "as the adult version" and added "we look at (TikTok) like a steppingstone to Triller".[13] He gets further quoted that the latter is due to the

---

[12] https://www.prnewswire.com/news-releases/triller-to-host-tyson-vs-jones-jr-press-conference-on-october-29th-at-1pm-et-301158927.html

[13] https://www.cnbc.com/2020/08/07/triller-on-being-tiktoks-rival-we-see-ourselves-as-the-adult-version.html

Triller's riskier content. Personally, I cannot perceive Triller to feature more risky content than TikTok, after all, a Twerk is a Twerk, or? Scan this QR-Code and judge for yourself.

I think this example was pretty out there, too. Or what do you think?

Figure 3. Tyson on Triller

Kavanaugh presented however a valid point with regards to TikTok's rather skewed user demographics towards the younger side. More than 50% of TikTok's users are reported to be below 34 years old and almost 26% between 18 and 24.[14] Note, these figures exclude users between the minimum specified age of 13 years to 18. This number can be expected to further skew the age average towards the younger side.

Thus, if Triller's strategy is to position itself on the slight upper end of that age group, to attract millennials and other more mature users through this focus on celebrities, remains to be seen. It is probably a very risky move, as TikTok has started to grow its own celebrities, which are almost all within Generation Z's demographical boundary. As such, it is questionable if these new breeds of celebrities, such as Charli d'amelio and her family, Addison Rae and many others will fully transition to Triller, once they and their user base matures. Most of these new stars have shown moves towards YouTube, Instagram and even towards TV-shows and podcasts.

Nevertheless, Triller announced in a September 2020 press release, that over 100 TikTok influencers, including the D'amelio family, have already joined Triller.[15] The in chapter 2 and 3 discussed monetization endeavors surely add to the potential attractiveness of Triller for commercially driven content creators

I guess one could say: they do follow the money!

---

[14] https://www.marketingcharts.com/digital/social-media-108342

[15] https://www.prnewswire.com/news-releases/triller-launches-crosshype-a-first-of-its-kind-brand-growth-program-combining-a-cpm-model-with-influencers-and-user-generated-content-forever-changing-brand-marketing-301136053.html

User base

Another obvious difference is TikTok's userbase, as compared to Triller. Although this is not a feature, but a developmental difference, it weighs heavy if one assumes that a TikTok ban in the US, or further countries, is unlikely. In such a case, the winner takes it all effect applies, which in the past has led to the dominance of apps and platforms in their respective category.[16] This concept assumes, that once a platform achieves a certain level of user growth, this marks a competitive tipping point. Think of Facebook some years back. Users started to join the platform despite their personal preferences, because family and friends were on it. This social pull effect expedites with the growth in users. The assumed global user base of TikTok, which is now probably close to the 800, or even 850 million users, stands thus in contrast to Triller's self-reported 250 million downloads and 100 million global users.[17] It has to be noted, that some question Triller's reported user numbers. One article discussing the potentially inflated user statistics can be accessed by scanning the following QR-Code.

---

[16] https://sloanreview.mit.edu/article/beyond-a-winner-takes-all-strategy-for-platforms/

[17] https://www.theverge.com/2020/10/2/21499177/tiktok-competitor-triller-monthly-active-users

For the sake of fairness, I would personally question all reported and non-verified user statistics of any platform or app that has a monetary interest attached to these numbers.

Usability

One of the biggest differences to me as a user and content creator is the usability (UX) of the TikTok app vs. the Triller app. TikTok, although prone for glitches and app-crashes in some of the recent releases, has a very intuitive app-interface. Shooting and editing videos is fairly easy and requires little effort for most users. Triller feels very similar by the looks of the user-interface, yet requires a little more in-app learning to be able navigate around the app. To name a difference, TikTok's FYP naming seems contextually intuitive. Triller's Trills page, although providing a very similar functionality, is based on a non-contextual naming convention. Further, Triller still seems a bit laggy in behavior and content loading, at least in my case using a 1Gbit line. Based on Trillers latest investment round and the growth of the company, one would expect these issues to be of lesser concern in the near future. Equally, creating a Triller video is not intuitive at first. Clicking on the create button, a user has to decide whether to create a music video or a social video. What is the difference? How would a user intuitively know? As an academic and as a marketer, I believe that Triller's own market perception and currently unprecise positioning strategy is to blame for the lack of usability. Once Triller's positioning is clear, being either a full fletched AI driven music video app, a short video social media platform, or something else, its UX will probably adapt to the target users of that strategy.

In the press

Triller has, as least to my knowledge and abilities to use online search, not had many negative mentions in the media. The probably most notable news around Triller center around the looming US ban of TikTok and thus the shift of users' focus on Triller. This has been a steady headline throughout the summer of 2020.[18]

With that, Triller welcomed popular TikTok creators who started to migrate to its platform. Amongst the earliest were Josh Richards, Noah Beck and Griffin Johnson.[19] Josh Richards even assumed the role of Triller's chief strategy officer, citing security concerns for his move towards Triller. All three remain however active on TikTok, attempting to move some of their massive following over to Triller. Nevertheless, appointing an 18-year-old to the role of chief strategy officer, is not a move one sees every day. Relying upon Richards' experience on social media, where he garnered millions of followers, does however make sense; if it wasn't for the contradiction of Triller's earlier discussed goal: to be the transitional follow-up, the grown-up version to TikTok. Looking at Richard's profile and his content, one could reasonably assume his followership to be rather young and predominantly female. See for yourself by scanning the following QR-Code to get to Richard's TikTok profile.

---

[18] https://www.scmp.com/yp/discover/entertainment/article/3095568/tiktok-stars-are-leaving-platform-rival-app-triller-over

[19] https://www.cnbc.com/2020/08/06/how-tiktok-star-josh-richards-got-20-million-followers.html

More on popular creators on Triller later. Other media mentions around Triller center mostly around two further topics.

First, the previously addressed rumor, that Triller is inflating its reported user numbers.[20] One has to say, if this holds true, it might leave a little, short-spurred dent in Triller's image. This image and market reputation has much benefited from Triller's efforts to treat user data with confidentiality and security, particularly in the US.

The other recent headline evolves around Triller seeking legal actions against TikTok in a patent infringement case. In a responding move TikTok filed a case against Triller for the loss in business caused by Triller's patent infringement accusations.[21] At the time of writing this book, the outcome of the above is still pending.

---

[20] https://techcrunch.com/2020/08/20/triller-threatened-to-sue-over-report-suggesting-it-inflated-its-downloads/

[21] https://www.cnbc.com/2020/10/29/tiktok-bytedance-sue-rival-triller.html

Alternatives to Triller

Can there be alternatives to Triller? Just kidding! There is a substitute for everything on the planet, no matter how good something is. Thus, there are also plenty of substitutes for Triller. To remain within the category of short video apps, I will primarily discuss Triller's app competition in this book.

The market for short-video apps, whether lip-syncing or storytelling focused, has proven interesting for many technology companies. Various companies, even the likes of Google and Facebook, have shown interest in the accelerating growth of short videos, mostly exhibited through the rise of TikTok.

Following, we will look at some notable direct competitors to Triller. The most noteworthy are: TikTok, Instagram Reels and YouTube Shorts.

TikTok

Trillers biggest competitor and the current market leader in the short video market is TikTok. TikTok is owned by parent-company ByteDance. ByteDance Ltd. was founded in 2012 by Yiming Zhang as a technology company.[22] Zhang is a former Microsoft engineer and one of China's many serial entrepreneurs. ByteDance is headquartered in Beijing, China and owns various subsidiaries and products. The most prominent products are:

- Toutiao (a Chinese news aggregation site)

---

[22] https://www.bytedance.com/en/

- Helo (an Indian Social Media app)
- Douyin (the Chinese version of TikTok)
- BaBe (an Indonesian news and content app), and
- TikTok.

In 2019, ByteDance was valued at over USD 78 billion, adding it to the global list of unicorns, firms worth USD 1 billion of more. Speculations about a potential IPO in Hong Kong have been looming since 2019. Up to the time of writing this book, ByteDance has denied any plans for public listing in the near future.[23]

Notable landmarks, relevant for this book, include:
- September 2016 - launch of Douyin in China
- May 2017 - launch of TikTok outside of China,
- November 2017 - acquisition of Musical.ly for USD 1 billion
- August 2018 - merger of the musical.ly platform with TikTok
- April 2019 – launch of Lark to enter the enterprise market

As of now, TikTok has a global monthly active user base of self-reported 700 million, out of which 100 million are in the US.[24] That marks an 800% growth in the US since 2018.

---

[23] https://www.reuters.com/article/us-bytedance-ipo/tiktok-owner-bytedance-says-it-has-no-immediate-hong-kong-ipo-plans-denies-ft-report-idUSKBN1X72B0

[24] https://www.cnbc.com/2020/08/24/tiktok-reveals-us-global-user-growth-numbers-for-first-time.html

TikTok has however not just gotten global attention through its rocket like growth numbers and being amongst the most downloaded apps of 2019 and 2020.[25] TikTok also made headlines through content and user censorship accusations,[26] a very lose data-handling policy and the attempt of the app to collect vast amounts of user data.[27] This has led the app to become the center of attention in the US – China tradewar, resulting in a looming ban of TikTok in the US.[28] As of now, this ban has been put on hold due to a potential acquisition of TikTok's US operations by Oracle and Wal-Mart.[29] Microsoft's bid was rejected in the process by TikTok. The outcome of the US presidential election and particularly the legal battle between TikTok and the US government is likely going to decide the fate of TikTok in the US. In the meantime, this positions Triller as a very interesting alternative to TikTok for many US users. As such, many popular creators have started to open Triller accounts, which has catapulted Triller to be the most downloaded app in August 2020.[30]

Compared to other competitors, TikTok's main competitive advantage, besides its now huge & global user base, is its very intuitive and minimalistic app design and its algorithm.

---

[25] https://wallaroomedia.com/blog/social-media/tiktok-statistics/

[26] https://www.theguardian.com/technology/2019/sep/25/revealed-how-tiktok-censors-videos-that-do-not-please-beijing

[27] https://www.thesun.co.uk/tech/11979917/tiktok-and-50-other-iphone-apps-spying-accusation/

[28] https://www.businessinsider.com/donald-trump-tiktok-ban-us-china-explained-in-30-seconds-2020-8?r=US&IR=T

[29] https://www.wsj.com/articles/microsoft-drops-out-of-bidding-for-tiktoks-u-s-operations-11600039821

[30] https://www.thejakartapost.com/life/2020/08/05/what-is-triller-the-app-that-is-overtaking-tiktok-in-the-app-store.html

TikTok's algorithm is largely unmatched in its ability to understand its users' behavior and content liking to serve an infinite stream of user focused content. YouTube, Facebook and many others have long focused on a user's friendship circle as a means to curate content. TikTok has gone a completely different route, which seems to work. At least so far. The agility of TikTok's management and thus the ability to quickly react to environmental changes is also unprecedented and requires some credit. This was exemplified through the creation of TikTok's EduTok learning initiative to counteract the apps first ban in India. Also, the appointment of an ex-Disney Manager as the global CEO, although short-lived in nature, marked a smart move during the accelerating US market expansion.

Instagram Reels

Facebook's first answer to TikTok was the launch of "Lasso" in November 2018. Lasso was exclusively launched in the US market. In early 2019, Lasso was reported to have 70.000 downloads, while TikTok clocked in a staggering 39.6 million app downloads in the same time period. Both estimates consider US downloads only.[31]

Instagram, acquired by Facebook in 2012,[32] has been experimenting since late 2019 with another TikTok clone in Brazil. Instagram's short-video answer to TikTok is called Reels.[33] Reels differs from Facebook's standalone attempt

---

[31] https://www.cnbc.com/2019/02/27/tiktok-is-staying-way-ahead-of-facebooks-lasso.html

[32] https://www.cnbc.com/2019/09/24/facebook-bought-instagram-because-it-was-scared-of-twitter-and-google.html

[33] https://techcrunch.com/2019/11/12/instagram-reels/

with Lasso, by allowing a deep integration with Instagram's story features. This opens up the opportunity of cross-promotions to Instagram's gigantic user base of over 1 billion monthly active users.[34] Reels was launched in mid 2020 in the US and is now also available in Europe.[35] If Reels can capture market share successfully remains to be seen. Based on a US user survey however, it appears that users do not perceive a difference between Reels and TikTok.[36] Thus Reels might be well positioned to capture TikTok users looking for an alternative. Its main advantage is Instagram's vast monetization potential, which has already led many creators to drive traffic from TikTok to their Instagram account. With Triller's current absence of advertising and thus direct platform monetization through views or ads, it remains to be seen if creators value the simplicity to monetize over their freedom to independently control brand relationships.

YouTube Shorts

On September 14, YouTube announced the launch YouTube Shorts.[37] This was a smart, yet seemingly desperate move by YouTube to become relevant in the war for 15 seconds of attention. Why do I say that? Well, YouTube is the undisputed king of video sharing. According to YouTube, it has over 2 billion monthly active users.[38] Only Facebook beats that

---

[34] https://about.instagram.com/about-us

[35] https://about.instagram.com/blog/announcements/introducing-instagram-reels-announcement

[36] https://www.forbes.com/sites/johnkoetsier/2020/09/07/87-of-tiktok-users-instagram-reels-is-basically-the-same/?sh=6f1f6f766967

[37] https://support.google.com/youtube/thread/71081044?hl=en

[38] https://www.youtube.com/about/press/

number with its 2.7 billion monthly active users, yet not in the same category.[39] However, YouTube differs much from Triller or TikTok. Let's find out how exactly!

First, curating a YouTube following takes a lot of effort and equally a lot of time. If we look at the most successful, or rising YouTube channels, we can almost tell the production value of their uploads. The probably most extreme example is Mr. Beast. Please scan the following QR-Code to get to Mr. Beast's YouTube channel. Trust me, you will be wowed!

The secret of Mr. Beasts success? The investment of YouTube revenue in content production. The average Mr. Beast video has probably a production value of USD 1-1.5 million! As an example, see the screenshot below in figure 4.

In this clip, Mr. Beast gave away USD 1 million to whoever kept his hand the longest on the pile of cash. This upload took probably weeks in planning, days in shooting and also days in editing.

---

[39] https://www.omnicoreagency.com/facebook-statistics/

Figure 4. Mr. Beast 1 Million Dollar in cash challenge

Casey Neistat, another successful YouTuber, once commented on the editing duration of his uploads. Neistat edits up to 8 hours per video.

Another factor is the time it takes on YouTube to grow a user base. Mr. Beast, who sports now over 45 million subscribers, started his channel in 2012. To contrast, Charli D'amelio has 95 million subscribers on TikTok, 8 million on YouTube and almost 6 million on Triller. The difference to Mr. Beast, Charli is now 16 and had her first YouTube post in late 2019. She experienced her hypergrowth through TikTok and was able to channel-convert her fame, almost effortlessly, to all other platforms, including YouTube. The bulk of her efforts? 15 second dance choreographies.

The launch of YouTube Shorts seems thus an effort to avoid the obsolescence of YouTube in the long run by missing to capture Generation Z and even Generation Alpha as new creators. After all, YouTube is only as strong as its content and this needs careful curation to continue to attract 2 billion monthly active users.

A genius move by YouTube was to launch YouTube shorts first in India. Why? TikTok just received its 2nd ban by the Indian government in mid 2020.[40] Thus millions of Indian TikTok users, who once marked TikTok's strongest market, were suddenly blocked from using TikTok. YouTube's answer: it's 15 second alternative. I would not call this innovative, but being at the right time at the right place!

Want to know more about YouTube Shorts? Scan this QR-Code to get to Google's Blog Update.

---

[40] https://techcrunch.com/2020/09/14/youtube-launches-its-tiktok-rival-youtube-shorts-initially-in-india/

Other noteworthy competitors

Dubsmash is another interesting competitor in the short video market. Yet chances are, you have never heard of Dubsmash before.[41,42] Rising to fame in 2015, Dubsmash almost completely disappeared in 2017. In late 2017, Dubsmash was relocated in a last attempt to save the app. It moved from Berlin to Brooklyn. After a year of reviving and fine-tuning the app, Dubsmash quietly rose to be a serious competitor, counting 1 billion monthly content views.

Likee,[43] *Kwai*[44] and *Firework*[45] complete the list, yet with lesser relevance; based on app-installations and their active monthly user-base. As of now, the market seems to suggest, that different short-video apps can co-exist. If this constellation continues, or if a market consolidation happens in the future, remains to be seen. Oh! And there is also *Byte*![46]

Further, one has to consider *Animoto*,[47] *Slidely*[48] and *Magisto*.[49] These companies are however more prone to be compared to Triller's video-editing core.

---

41 https://dubsmash.com

42 https://techcrunch.com/2020/01/31/dubsmash-songs/

43 https://likee.com

44 https://www.kwai.com/about/

45 https://fireworktv.com

46 https://byte.co

47 https://animoto.com

48 http://slide.ly

49 https://www.magisto.com

Chapter 2: the App

This chapter describes the Triller app from an interface perspective and provides insights into the video creation, sharing and viewing experience. Please note, that Triller is a dynamic organization and thus its app is likely to constantly evolve. Thus, some features might have been added or changed since the writing of this book.

Interface

The Triller user interface is quite clean and shows a strong resemblance to the one of TikTok, as do most short video applications.

Opening Triller, the app opens its content feed. This is shown in figure 5. The content feed is split in "Following" and "Trills". "Following" shows content from other Triller user you follow, while "Trills" displays a curated content feed. Triller's curated content does not play to my very taste, but other than that, the content feed displays very similar interface and interaction options than other apps.

Figure 5. Triller content screen

Switching to the "Following" content feed, displays in my very case no content, as I have not yet followed other Triller users. See figure 6 for details. If you do follow Triller users, their content stream will appear under "Following", the rest remains as with the "Trills" content feed.

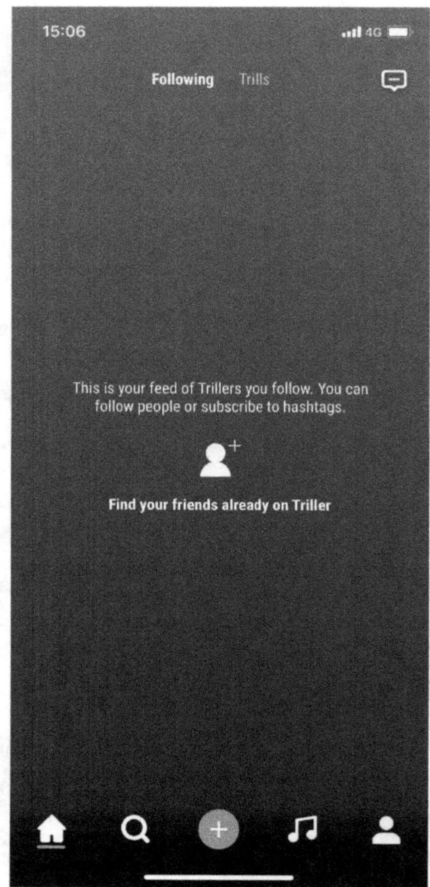

Figure 6. Content from followers

Watching Triller content, as displayed in figure 5, allows you to interact via "Likes", "Comments", "Messaging" the user and "Sharing" the video. Other than that, you can of course tap on the used music on the bottom right to get to the soundtrack's page, tap on the used hashtags or the user's profile. Highlighted in red is the option to follow the user; Triller made this very easy and obvious.

Sharing a clip, feels very slow. In my very case, using a 4G, 5G or even a highspeed network, I am always faced with a loading screen before the sharing menu appears. See figure 7.

Figure 7. Loading screen

While a loading screen is not the end of the world, it feels overly long to wait a few seconds, if the content you consume is only 15 seconds long. The average loading time of the sharing option screen seems to be around 5 to 10 seconds in my case. Once you tap on sharing, there is no return but to wait until the seemingly infinite loading time is over. Triller could do better here!

Once the sharing options have loaded, you have various options to forward, share or download the clip.

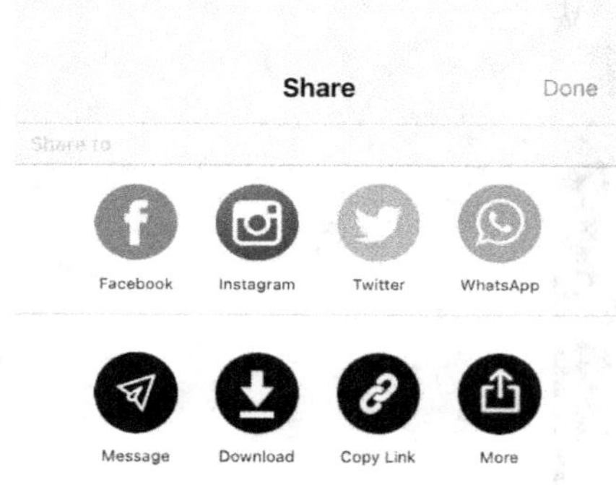

Figure 8. Sharing options

For my taste, these options are all that is needed for most users. If you tap on "More", your phones sharing options open up. These double some of the previous features, but are a nice touch by Triller. See figure 9.

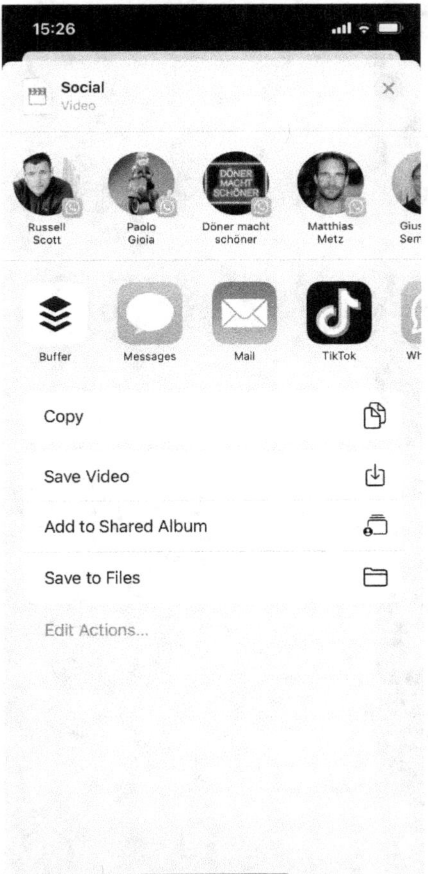

Figure 9. Advanced sharing options

Going back to the "Home" screen, we can also see the "Search", "Create", "Music" and "Profile" icon. Most are self-explanatory and require only a tap to understand their features.

Nevertheless, let's have a brief look at each. See figure 10 for the "Search" or "Discover" functionality.

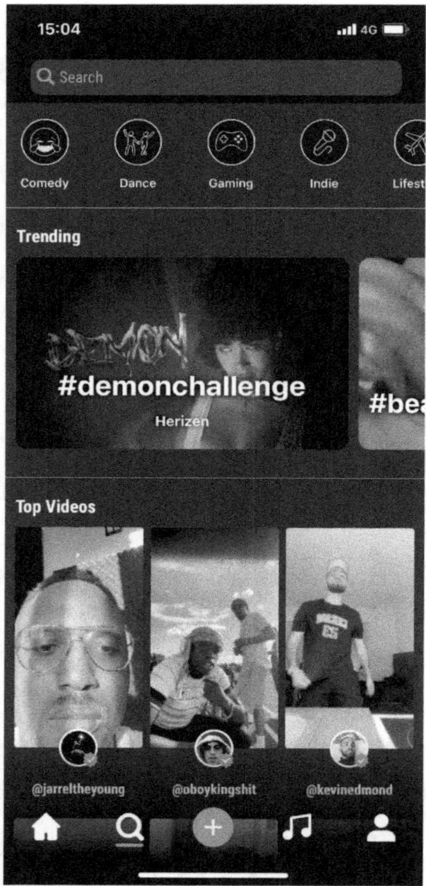

Figure 10. Search

Tapping the "Search" or "Discover" icon lets you explore videos by genre, such as comedy, dance, gaming and so on. It lets you find trending challenges and of course currently trending videos. On the very top, you are also offered a search field, to search for anything that comes to mind. Likely, you will find it!

Tapping on "Create", the red icon in the middle, opens the creator's view. See figure 11.

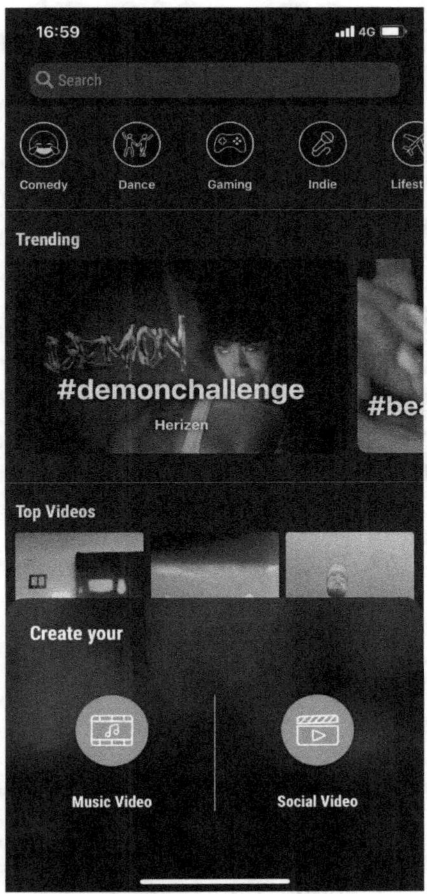

Figure 11. Create

There you have a choice between creating a "Music Video" or a "Social Video". The latter lets you further define the category of "Social Video" you aim to create. As explained previously, "Music Videos" begin with you selecting a soundtrack, recording your videos and letting Triller work the magic. "Social Videos" on the other hand give you more editing freedom, but do not (yet) allow the selection of a soundtrack as an ambience to your creation. You'll also find plenty of effects and filters to get creative. Covering all these features makes little sense, your best bet to become Triller proficient: JUST DO IT!

If you require some help, I suggest the following tutorial which runs you step by step through the creation of a video.

And? Did you create your first video?

Moving on, if you tap the "Music" symbol, see figure 12, you get to Triller's large catalogue of available music titles. Again, you'll find sorting criteria on top, starting with featured and trending music. Tapping on a category, shows the corresponding music in a listed view, highlighting the numerical view-count of soundtracks. This will give you an idea of the sound's popularity. Tapping on a song, let's you choose between listening to the song and using the song for your next "Music video" creation. See figure 13. Unfortunately, Triller does not yet allow to save a song, or a video for that matter, in a "favorite list" as TikTok does. This is a truly handy feature and sometimes much needed if you continue watching other users' creations but aim to record or fine-tune your video only later.

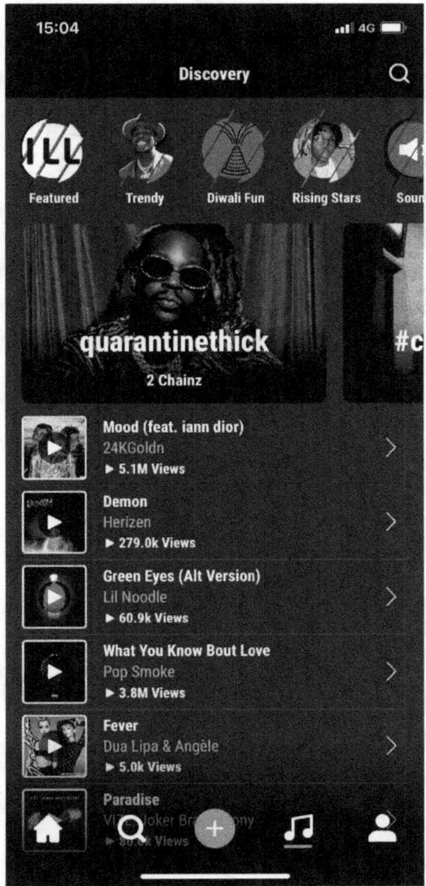

Figure 12. Music

Also, you can view the top videos and creators who have used this song, as well as the latest uploads on Triller. This can also be used as a mean to measure the popularity of a song.

Attention: do not forget, that some popular creators perform to certain songs as part of a sponsored engagement. The music industry has long understood the power of short video platforms to hype titles, push artists and have songs in the trending charts. Just be aware of this!

Figure 13. A song

Going back to "Home" or your feed, you see a speech bubble type symbol on the top right. Tapping there leads you to your "Activity Center". See figure 14.

Figure 14. Activity Center

Your activity center displays all interactions with your uploads. In my case, there are currently none to display. On the top right, you find the "Message" symbol. Tapping on that takes you to your inbox, see figure 15.

Figure 15. Inbox

There you see direct messages received from people you are connected with under "Following" and everybody else's under "Others". This feature requires probably no further explanation.

Let's go to your own profile. Tap the "Profile" symbol on the bottom right. This will take you to your personal Triller profile, see figure 16.

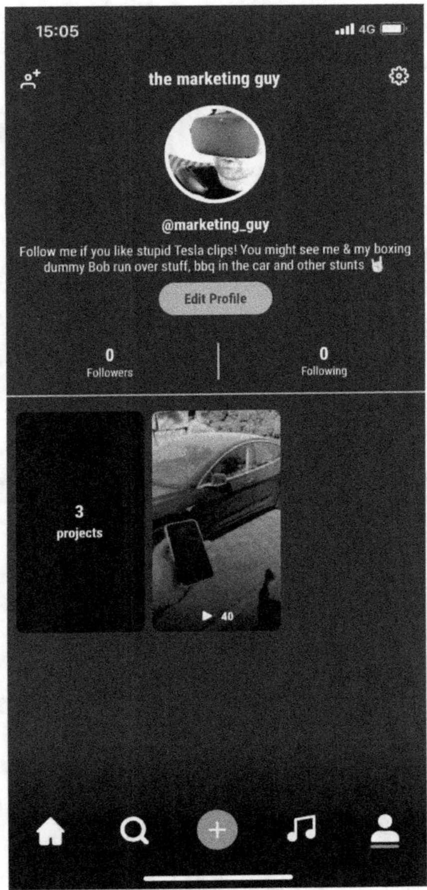

Figure 16. Profile

In my very case, you see I have 3 projects in my work in progress (wip) folder and 1 completed social video, with 40 views. To contrast, the very same clip got me a little over 2 million views on TikTok. Having said that, I have not put much effort in creating native Triller content. Why? Time reasons! With 2 young kids and various professional engagements, you can only do that much. Again, I'm not an influencer and don't strive to be one. Still, comparatively, I s..ck at Triller and could have done better!

On the top left, you see the option to "Fiend Friends", see figure 17.

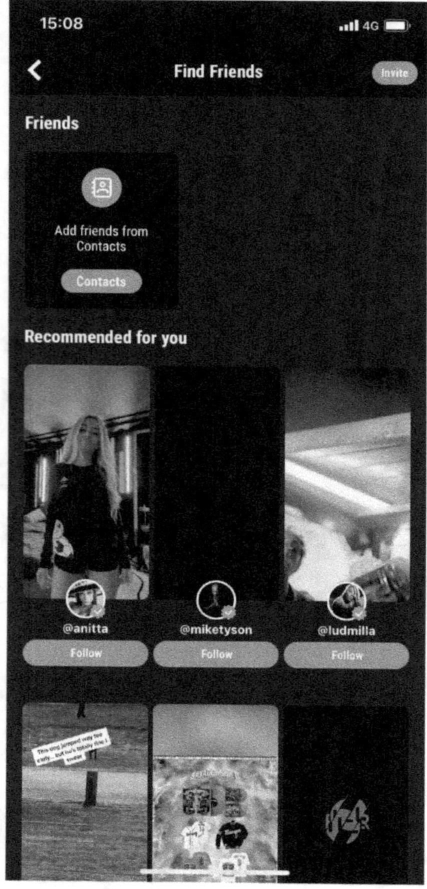

Figure 17. Add users

You have the option to look for friends in your personal contact list or add "friends" as recommended by Triller. Adding a friend equals you following another user. I wouldn't mind however, to claim Mike Tyson to be a personal friend of mine. If you tap on invite, see figure 18, you have the further option to send either a text message or an E-Mail, encouraging friends to a) join Triller and b) follow you.

Adding WhatsApp or other social networks, or having a personal invite link, would be a nice touch to make sharing your Triller profile just a tad easier.

Figure 18. Invite

Further, being in your profile view, refer back to figure 16, you can view your own creations, edit your profile or edit your Triller preferences.

Let's start with your own videos. View an upload by tapping on it, see figure 19.

Figure 19. Videos

The only difference to other clips is, that you spot 3 dots on the right of your name and video description. Tapping on the 3 dots opens up a menu that lets you "Edit video details", change its accessibility in "Make the video private", "Share" and "Delete". See figure 20.

Figure 20. Video edit

Sharing and deleting the clip is self-explanatory. But the other 2 options are of higher relevance. "Making the video private" restricts the public accessibility of the video. Enabling this, will make the clip only viewable to you. Unfortunately, you cannot restrict video accessibility to only your followers, which is probably a needed feature for the protection of younger users. "Edit video details", see figure 21, provides you the option to alter your creation's title and description. This might be relevant to tweak hashtags in use.

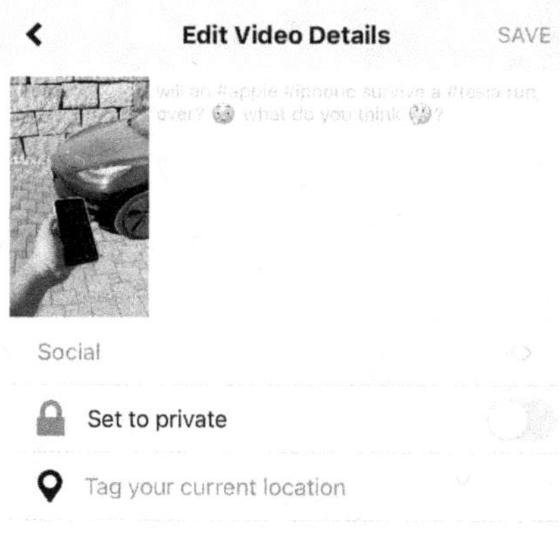

Figure 21. Edit video

As you can see in figure 21, you can also adjust your video's accessibility under "Edit video details". You can however not edit the video itself post upload. I believe this would be a tremendous feature if users could adjust their creations post upload. Also, in the case of a "Social video", you can change the genre. See figure 22.

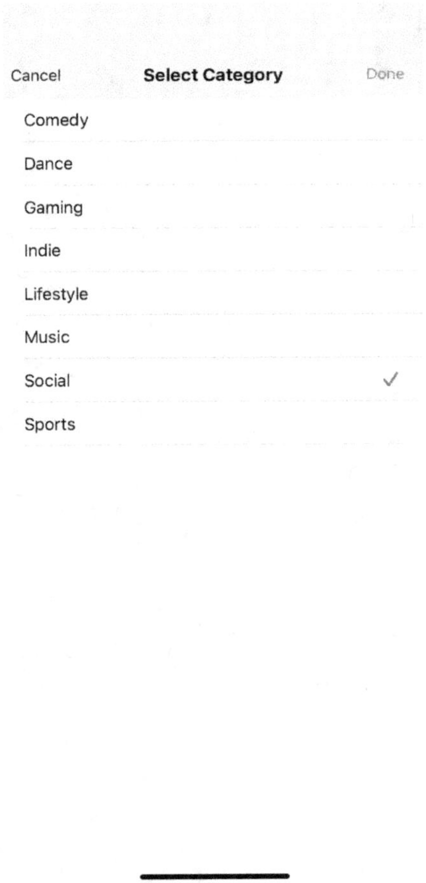

Cancel　　**Select Category**　　Done

Comedy

Dance

Gaming

Indie

Lifestyle

Music

Social　　　　　　　　　　✓

Sports

Figure 22. Change genre

If the impact of the genre has a true impact on your reach or views, is currently unclear. It seems to however only matter to categorize your uploads for the "Discovery" page.

Going back to your profile, you can further edit your profile's details. See figure 23.

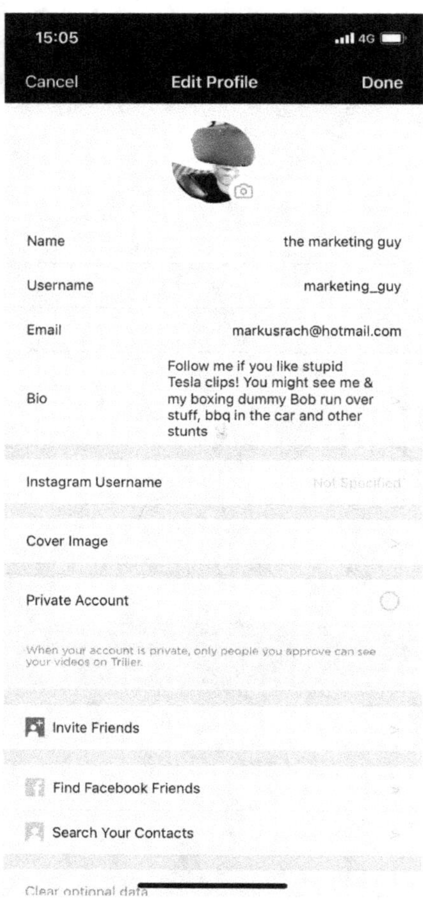

Figure 23. Profile details

Since Figure 23 is self-explanatory, let's look into the Triller's preference settings. See figure 24 and figure 25 for details.

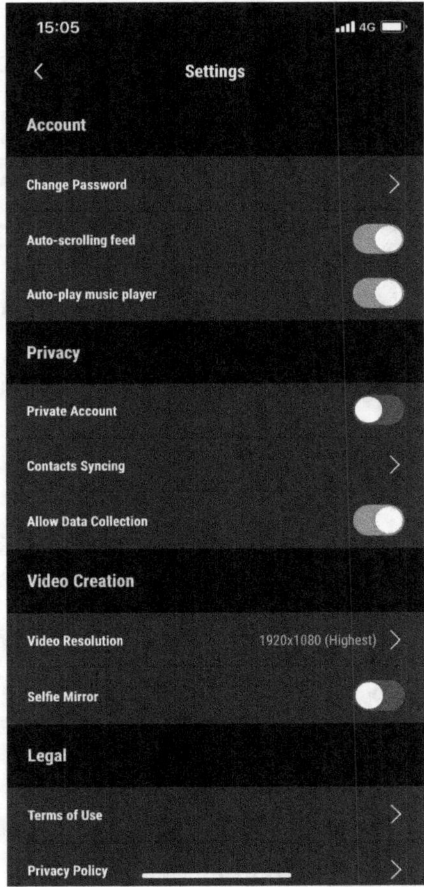

Figure 24. Triller Preferences 1

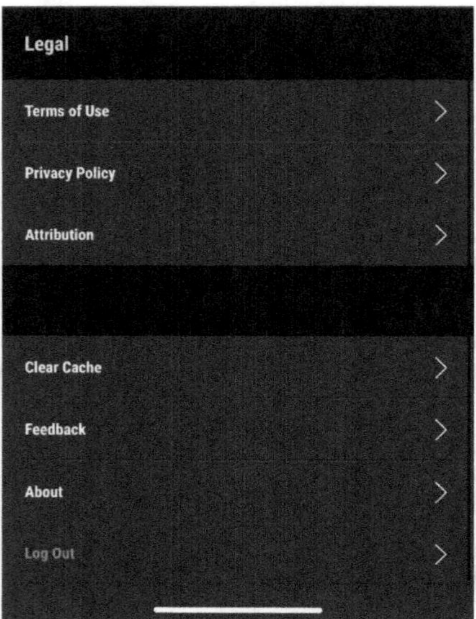

Figure 25. Triller Preferences 2

Triller's preference settings are minimalistic at this point. You can access the most important settings yet changing the video resolution is probably a setting of secondary importance to many. What I am missing in the preference settings is an option to restrict the download of videos by other users. This might a relevant feature for both private users, as well as brands, to somewhat restrict the use of their content. Be warned, screen-capturing technology allows of course to locally store and edit content independent of any app-settings. Nevertheless, TikTok provides the just mentioned feature.

Before you continue, I suggest making yourself familiar with the Triller user-interface.

Suggestions for creators

As said in the very beginning of this book, it is not meant as a resource for creators or aspiring influencers. There are other resources channeled at the very needs, that I neglect to address, or cannot address.

However, based on my experience using TikTok and Triller, considering the limited availability of resources to do so, mainly time, I have some suggestions to consider.

1. With great power, comes great responsibility!
No! I'm not suggesting that you are Spiderman, but equally to Spiderman, you hold great power. You inspire others! Use this impact for good! Although it is understandable that you might have monetary interests, just be aware of the impact your suggestions and posts have. As a bare minimum, please follow the FTC's regulations!

Be the superhero, which your followers see in you!

2. Use your resources wisely!

From a creator's perspective and unless you have a professional management, which not too many creators have, you need to make the best use of the resources you have. The most valuable resource of all is time! We all have 24 hours any given day and you have to likely split that time between various platforms you need to feed with content. Be aware of this and try to follow a content creation scheme to let you maximize your output within your resource constraints. An important aspect of this is content recycling. I'm not suggesting copying Dunkin' Donuts, by uploading your TikTok's to Triller, but by filming content with your phone's native camera app. This allows you to repurpose this content on various platforms, thus you only need one creative and one good take to upload to both TikTok and Triller, if not more. Just look at what Gary Vaynerchuck is doing, nobody masters content recycling any better.

3. Build a consistent brand!

Find your niche and develop that niche carefully. Make sure to spend some time to rethink your niche strategy. Posting a funny joke is great, but do you have enough funny jokes to keep that going with future posts? If you look at most of the leading popular creators, their niche offers an infinite pool of content ideas. Whether these are choreographed dance routines to trending music, singing songs, or telling fact-based events, make sure to discover your niche early on. Algorithms do not like change of content, thus changing your niche might impact the spread of your content on almost any platform.

Brands on Triller

Some notable brands have already started engaging on Triller. It should be no surprise to find major music labels, such as Sony Music or Universal Music on Triller. Other notable brands include McDonalds, Chipotle, Bang Energy, Red Bull and Dunkin' Donuts. See figures 26, 29 and 31 for details.

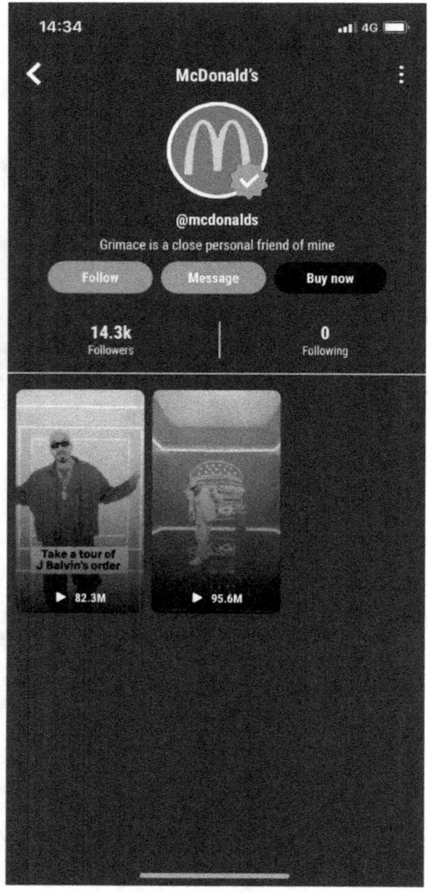

Figure 26. McDonalds Triller

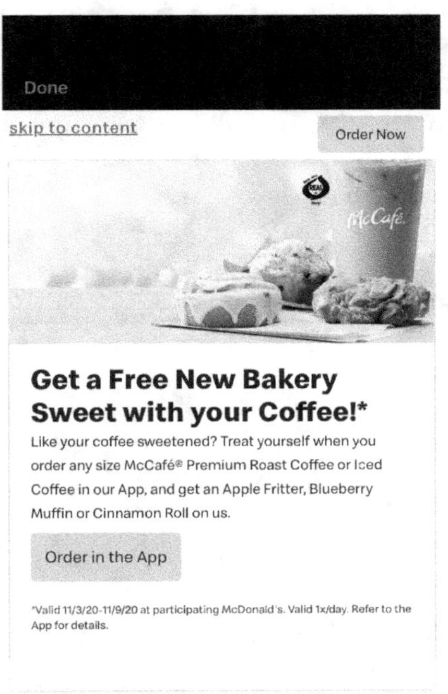

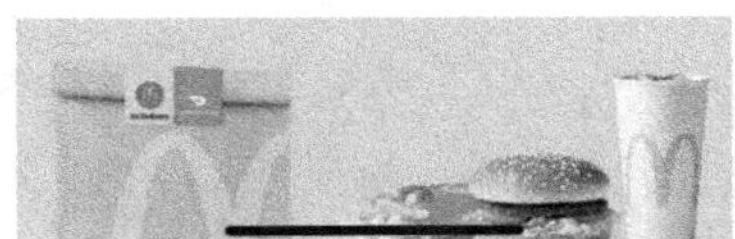

Figure 27. McDonalds Triller buy now

McDonalds integrated its menu and thus an e-commerce application into Triller. Smart! Instant conversion. I'm definitely loving it 😃!

Notable are the two pieces of content, featuring over 80 million and 90 million views. Impressive! Even for TikTok standards. McDonald's, which just recently joined Triller launched its account with a partnership with reggaeton singer

J Balvin.[50] It seems to work! Yet follower numbers are still miniscule, with 14.3k for a brand like McDonalds. To contrast, McDonalds has a following of 467.2K on TikTok, see figure 28.

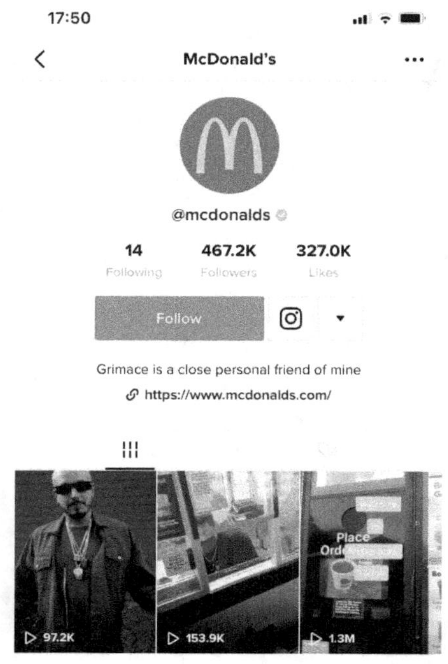

Figure 28. McDonald's TikTok

[50] https://digiday.com/media/were-at-the-crux-of-it-how-tiktok-rival-triller-is-brashly-pitching-advertisers/

As it seems, the account was also created in October, at least the first upload was featured on the 5th October 2020. One needs to wonder why the number of followers and the number of views differs so dramatically. Does Triller already guarantee views for on-platform partnership?

The next featured brand is Chipotle, refer to figure 29.

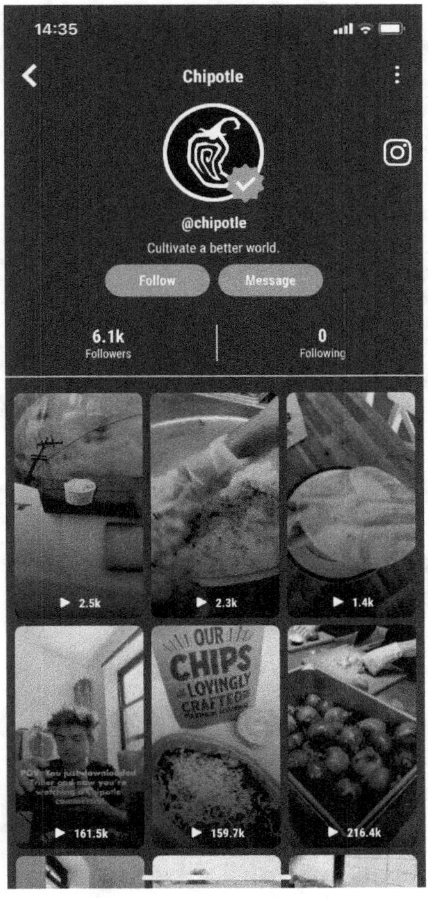

Figure 29. Chipotle Triller

On TikTok, Chipotle sports 1.3 million followers and 114 uploads. However, Chipotle ran already multiple TikTok challenges, such as the "Boorito" challenge, which alone features 4.1 billion hashtag views on TikTok, see figure 30.

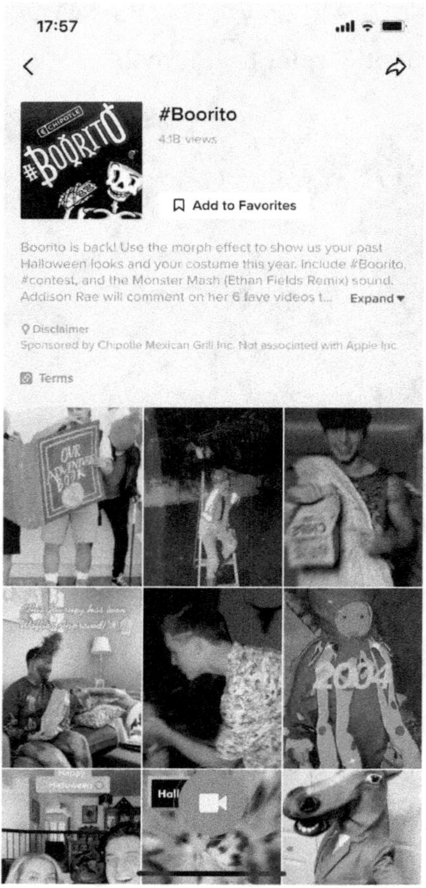

Figure 30. Boorito Challenge on TikTok

Thus, there is room to grow for Chipotle on Triller. The brand needs to probably find its way to create equally engaging content and paid features to gain users' attention.

Red Bull is usually a brand that experiments early on new apps and platforms. Thus, it is no surprise, to also see Red Bull on Triller. Yet, the brand who got global attention through its stratosphere stunt in 2012, displays again a fairly low number of followers. To contrast, Red Bull has 4.9 million followers on TikTok, and that doesn't include the brand's many additional country accounts, see figure 32.

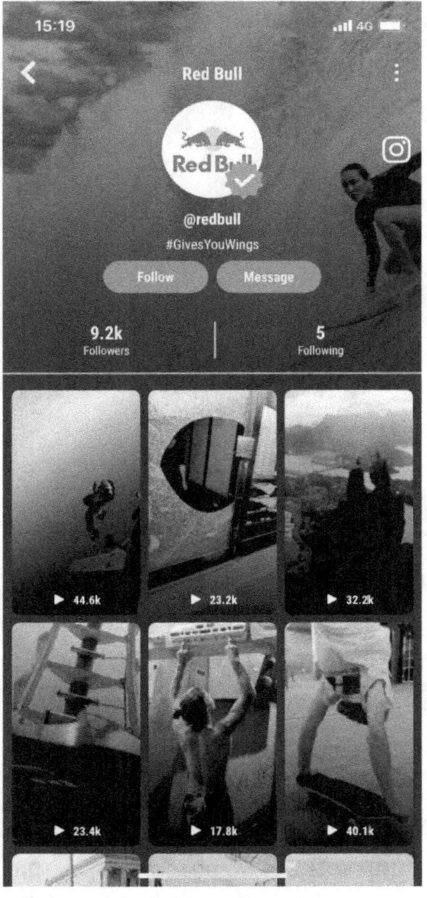

Figure 31. Red Bull Triller

Figure 32. Red Bull country accounts on TikTok

Red Bull's content split seems to pay off, there is no other brand, to my knowledge, with more combined followers on TikTok.

The next brand to mention is Bang Energy. Why? Bang Energy is a brand, although unknown to many, that aggressively used influencer promotions on TikTok to gain attention. If it replicates this on Triller, it is likely to thrive on the platform, too.

Figure 33. Bank Energy

Bang Energy features 1 million followers on TikTok, but does not show the verified checkmark, which it got already assigned on Triller.

Dunkin' Donuts is probably my favorite transactionally focused brand of 2020. On Triller, Dunkin' Donuts, shows a total of 125 followers. Screenshot date: 8th November 2020. View numbers are virtually non-existent, but the account has been verified. See the famous blue checkmark?

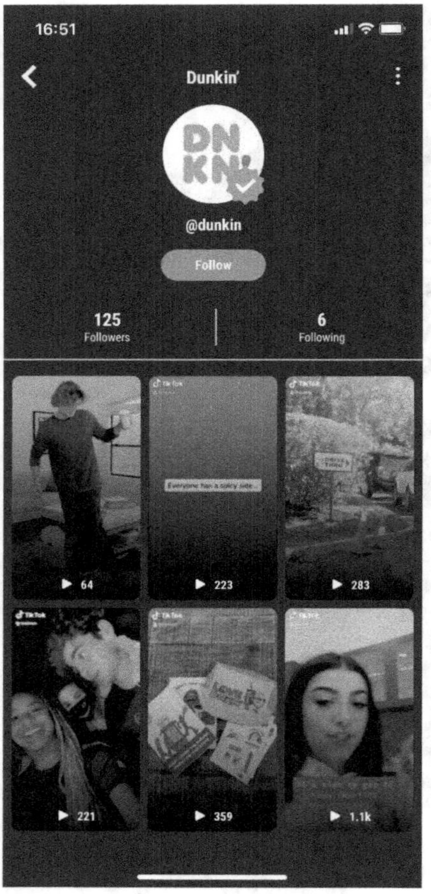

Figure 34. Dunkin' Donuts

Dunkin' Donuts put seemingly no effort into its Triller presence, which is probably one of the reasons for its mediocre success. The brand ran a partnership with the most followed person on TikTok, Charli D'amelio, that saw the brand to receive a 20% revenue spike in day 1 and over 45% on day 2. On Triller, the Dunkin' Donuts team uploaded their downloaded TikTok clips, even featuring the TikTok logo, see figure 35.

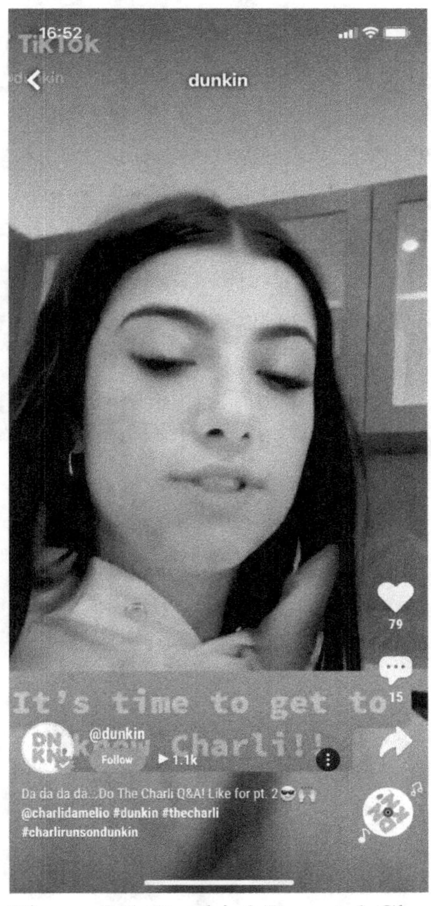

Figure 35. Dunkin' Donuts' Charli content

In my opinion, this screams for Dunkin' Donuts to receive the absolute "no effort" award of 2020.[51]

So, what should brands do on Triller? I believe, the absolute minimum investment of a brand should be to secure its brand name on the app. Other than that, brands need to understand that Triller is not TikTok. Triller has its own feel, its slightly different culture and a much deeper integration of music into its very core. This is likely to change with more and more users swapping over from TikTok. Nevertheless, in most cases, native content will beat repurposed content from other apps. Shown examples display this effect. With only seconds to gain attention and engagement, brands need to understand how to create engaging content on each platform. This marks a learning that holds true for Facebook, as it does for TikTok and now for Triller. I strongly believe that brands should use this opportunity and invest into their Triller presence. Regardless of TikTok's future, Triller is poised to become a strong player in the short video market, or the social streaming market. If history has taught us one thing, it's that the early bird catches the worm. This applied to the early accounts on TikTok and will apply to the early accounts, that put the necessary effort in, on Triller.

Brand managers: get your head around the social streaming opportunity Triller offers. This is somewhat unique and can create amazing brand storytelling opportunities. More on this later!

---

[51] https://www.tmz.com/2020/09/23/charli-damelio-dunkin-donuts-drink-cold-brew-sales-boost/

Want to become an influencer?

Did you know that the dream to become an influencer has overtaken the traditional job aspiration of the astronaut?[52] Not even SpaceX and the real-life Tony Stark, Elon Musk, could keep the little kids' dream to become an astronaut alive. If Musk cannot do, nobody can.

But what is so sexy about being an influencer? Being followed by millions? Receiving millions or even billions of likes? Ok! If you receive 7.6 billion likes for your channel, like Charli D'amelio on TikTok, that has to somewhat raise your self-esteem. For perspective reasons, our planet's population has been estimated at 7.8 billion in 2020.[53]

But could there be more than that? Yes, you got it! The only green is money and the life influencers' portray on social media reeks of fame, money, toys, cars and beautiful houses for seemingly no effort. Who wouldn't want that?

Mega influencers like Kim Kardashian and the king of Instagram, Dan Bilzerian, top the charts for the public portrayal of their life. See for yourself by scanning the following QR-Codes.

---

[52] https://www.cnbc.com/2019/07/19/more-children-dream-of-being-youtubers-than-astronauts-lego-says.html

[53] https://en.wikipedia.org/wiki/World_population

Dan Bilzerian[54]

Kim Kardashian[55]

Bilzerian, featuring over 32 million followers on Instagram and Kardashian, featuring 191 million followers, are however only the tip of the iceberg. Bilzerian is currently in the headlines for potentially financing his lavish lifestyle, as portrayed on Instagram, through his company's expenses.[56] Maybe the life of influencers isn't all that glossy and shiny as it seems on Instagram, or other platforms. It is also a hard job, that requires constant posting, constantly raising the bar to gain attention and the careful curation of your own brand. Not many influencers sustain this over time. In fact, a study by Prof Bärtl, from the Offenburg University of Applied Sciences, found while assessing YouTube channels, that 85% of the

---

[54] https://www.forbes.com/sites/chrisroberts/2020/07/09/dan-bilzerian-is-a-renter/?sh=1a048c4d7df5

[55] https://www.theguardian.com/lifeandstyle/2020/oct/21/kim-kardashian-west-at-40-how-the-queen-of-social-media-changed-the-world

[56] https://seekingalpha.com/article/4384157-dan-bilzerian-gives-ignite-huge-boost-troubles-continue-behind-facade

traffic went to only 3% of the channels.[57] Put differently, over 96% of YouTubers wouldn't make enough money, to get over the US federal poverty line of USD 12'140. Yet the dream to get rich posting content on social media lives on with 86% of Generation Z.[58]

For a fun, but interesting read, I recommend dwelling into the book of Brooke Erin Duffy, an Assistant Professor of Communication at Cornell University. Scan the following QR-Code to get to Duffy's book "(Not) Getting Paid to Do What You Love: Gender, Social Media, and Aspirational Work".

Btw. fun fact, the most followed person on Instagram, is not Kim Kardashian. Its Portugal's own: Cristiano Ronaldo with over 240 million followers, see figure 36! WOW! That makes Ronaldo the mega influencer of the mega influencers.

---

[57] https://scinapse.io/papers/2784178595

[58] https://www.cnbc.com/2019/11/08/study-young-people-want-to-be-paid-influencers.html

Figure 36. Cristiano Ronaldo's Instagram profile

With that, it is very refreshing to see, that sponsored posts on Ronaldo's feed are being clearly marked as sponsored content. Refer to figure 37.

Figure 37. Sponsored content

Unfortunately, in the world of short video formats, not all influencers adhere to marking sponsored posts as branded content or advertising. The Federal Trade Commission (FTC) issues regularly updates on the disclosure requirements for social media posts by influencers. See an extract, as well as the QR-Code to get to the relevant FTC site, below.

"If you endorse a product through social media, your endorsement message should make it obvious when you have a relationship ("material connection") with the brand. A "material connection" to the brand includes a personal, family, or employment relationship or a financial relationship – such as the brand paying you or giving you free or discounted products or services.

Telling your followers about these kinds of relationships is important because it helps keep your recommendations honest and truthful, and it allows people to weigh the value of your endorsements.

As an influencer, it's your responsibility to make these disclosures, to be familiar with the Endorsement Guides, and to comply with laws against deceptive ads. Don't rely on others to do it for you."[59]

I strongly recommend brands & influencers to adhere to the FTC's regulations.

---

[59] https://www.ftc.gov/tips-advice/business-center/guidance/disclosures-101-social-media-influencers

Influencers on Triller

Triller has its own breed of influencers, although of course, many faces seem familiar from TikTok. Charli D'amelio, the queen of TikTok has joined Triller in September 2020.[60] See figure 38 for Charli's Triller profile

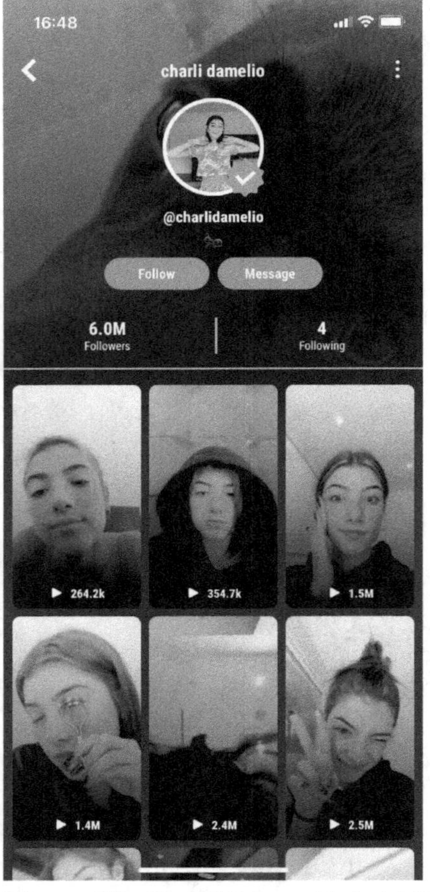

Figure 38. Charli D'amelio's Triller

[60] https://www.theverge.com/2020/9/15/21438111/charli-damelio-tiktok-triller-app-rival-dixie-marc-heidi

On Triller, Charli already sports a whopping 6 million followers. Not bad for repurposing content, although one has to give Charli credit, at least she repurposed native camera footage used for TikTok also on Triller. She surely has put more effort into her posts than Dunkin' Donuts. The spill-over effect from her almost 100 million followers strong TikTok seems massive, see figure 39.

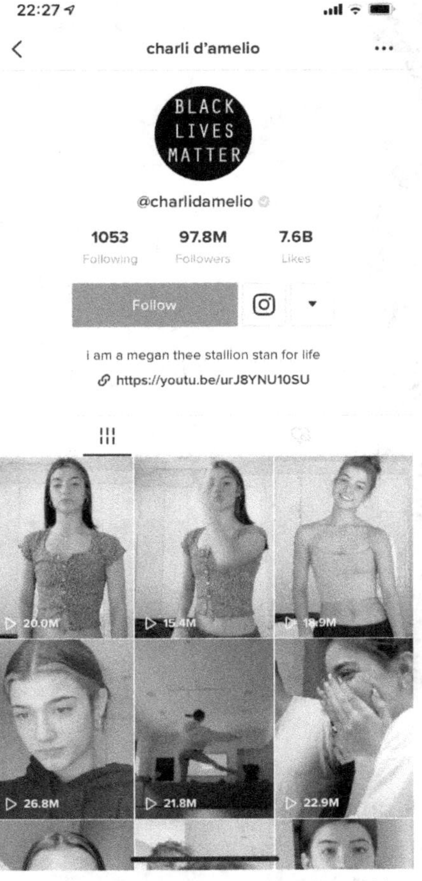

Figure 39. Charli D'amelio TikTok account

Going back to Triller, it is clearly notable, that Charli's activity rate lacks behind that of TikTok. This is also visible by looking at her following only 4 accounts, see figure 40.

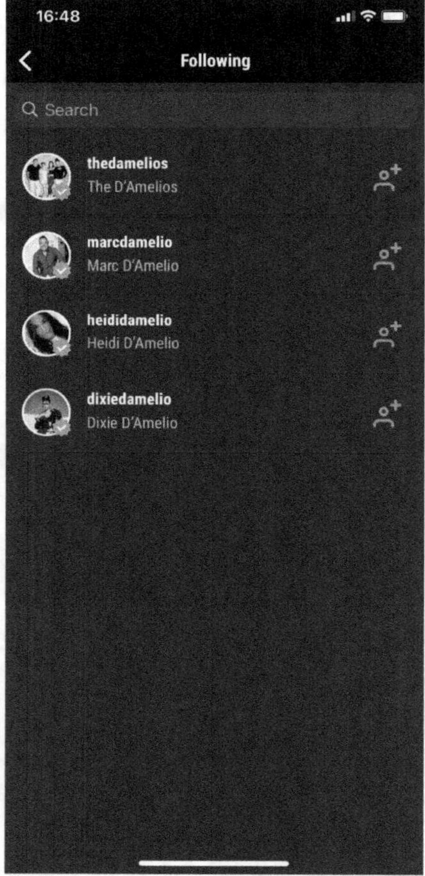

Figure 40. Charli's Following

Her following include the D'amelio's family account, her sister's and her parents'. It is probably fair to say, that we are witnessing the birth of the next Kardashian clan. Expect the D'amelios to have their own TV-show and to become the new face of America's reality TV. This is my bet, let's see if I have this right! For those who do not know Charli D'amelio, she is a US teenager, who became TikTok famous for her dance routines. She took over the reign on TikTok from Loren Gray in early 2020 and has led the TikTok charts since. As it seems, the spillover effect from her TikTok accounts replicates this leaderboard experience 1:1 on Triller. Charli has done various brand deals with brands like Dunkin's Donuts, Prada, Hollister[61] and others. She has also launched a makeup line with Morphe.[62] With all of this, Charli and her entire family, portrait the transactional nature of the influencer relationship to the core. The family has essentially turned into walking billboards, advertising to their very loyal, very young and very advertising illiterate followers. More on this later!

Fun fact, the D'amelio family has, combined on all channels, over 200 million followers; that is more followers than votes in the 2020 US election.[63]

Charli's sister, Dixie D'amelio, see figure 42, has equally materialized her fame into brand partnerships and the release of her own song "Be Happy". At the time of writing this book, "Be Happy" shows an impressive 91.8 million views on YouTube. Double-WOW! Although music is obviously very much subject to personal taste, one could discuss if Dixie's raw talent got the song to become that popular, or if it's the

---

[61] https://www.hollisterco.com/shop/eu/girls-charli-and-dixie-edit?originalStore=us

[62] https://www.insider.com/charli-dixie-damelio-makeup-morphe-date-products-line-2020-7

[63] https://www.cbsnews.com/news/joe-biden-popular-vote-record-barack-obama-us-presidential-election-donald-trump/

power of the family's 200 million followers, to whom the song was promoted to. As a YouTube user puts it, see figure 41.

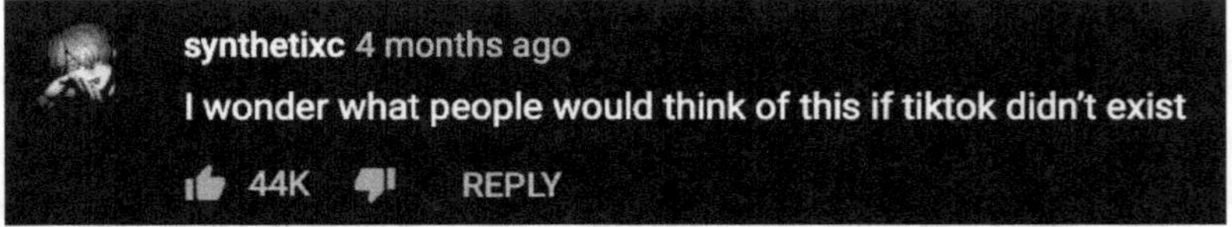

Figure 41. YouTube comment.

Figure 42. Dixi D'amelio's Triller

Dixie's TikTok account features 43.1 million followers. Further, Noah Beck, another famous face from TikTok, with over 19 million followers has also joined Triller, as mentioned earlier. Refer to figure 43.

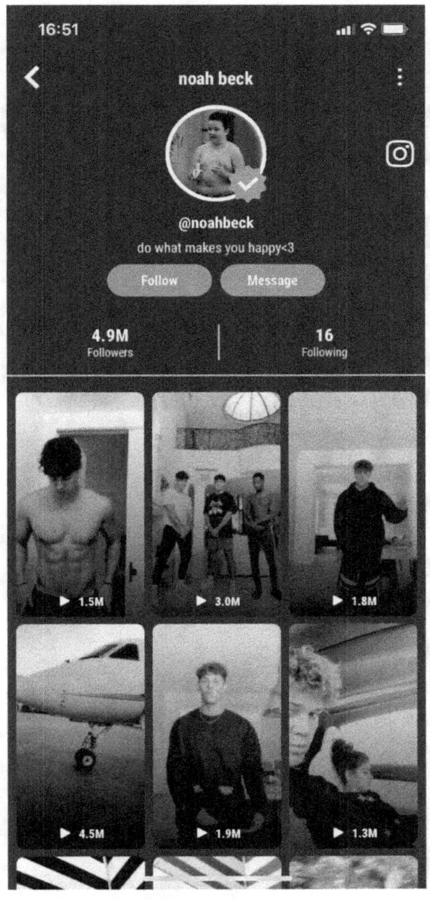

Figure 43. Noah Beck

It has to be noted, that the number two most followed account on TikTok, that of Addison Rae, another female featuring mainly dance choreographies, has not yet opened a public

Triller account. On TikTok however, Addison Rae has an impressive 69 million followers. A different influencer to mention, is the social media expert, agency owner and investor Gary Vaynerchuck, see figure 44.

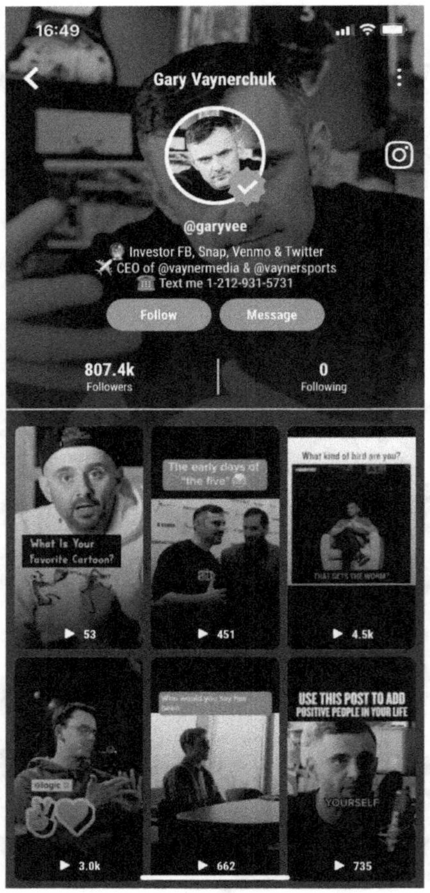

Figure 44. Gary Vee

Gary Vee is known for his extreme content recycling and over present nature on social media. I believe that it is fair to say, that his Triller account displays the opposite of what social media should be about. A broadcast channel with no interest to connect, share, exchange or engage with other users. Sporting a 0-following count, sends that message! I guess somebody had to say it!

Loren Gray was the long-time most followed account on TikTok, until Charli took the reins. Her Triller however lacks much behind her TikTok success, see figure 45.

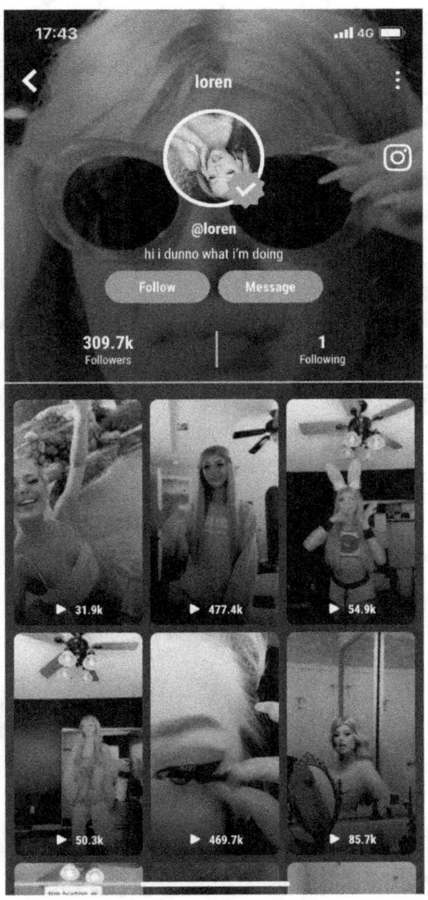

Figure 45. Loren (Gray)

With just over 300'000 followers, Loren Gray seems to struggle to attract the equal attention of other large TikTok creators on Triller. Her TikTok account shows 49.1 million followers, although her growth has seemingly slowed over the last couple of months. Does this hint towards a shorter lifespan of mega influencers on these platforms? Time will probably tell. TikTok's latest rising star, a creator named Bella Poarch, who got overnight famous through a headshake which also resulted in one of the biggest cyber-bullying cases of 2020, has also not yet joined Triller. Her account, which was largely unknown before her famous post on the 18th August 2020, features now over 41 million followers. Scan the following QR-Code to see her 513 million view strong post, that made her famous on TikTok.

Looking at the mentioned trend of creator spillover from TikTok to Triller, I have no doubt that users will follow and further push Triller up the short video app charts.

Chapter 3: Marketing & Safety

This chapter discusses marketing tactics around Triller, as well as user safety features. Both are relevant to brands to understand boundaries and opportunities. They are equally relevant to users to understand potential mechanics at work.

Marketing on Triller

At the time of writing this book, Triller did not yet provide advertising opportunities on its platform.[64] This does actually feel refreshing; yet Triller is still, despite its age of over 5 years, in an early growth phase in the short video sharing world. This is due to the previously discussed transition from a pure AI-powered video editing app to what Triller is now. Triller is encouraging brands to directly partner with creators on its platform. This is also a move, that one needs to understand as part of a platform's growth strategy. If creators perceive Triller as another potential stream of income, interest in the app will increase, particularly from popular creators transitioning to Triller from other apps.

In September 2020, Triller announced the launch of a new marketing service called "Crosshype".[65] Crosshype is probably best described by Triller's on press release.

---

[64] https://www.contagious.com/news-and-views/is-social-streaming-app-triller-the-tonic-advertisers-are-looking-for

[65] https://www.contagious.com/news-and-views/is-social-streaming-app-triller-the-tonic-advertisers-are-looking-for

"...This first-to-market "Crosshype" platform allows influencers to offer a complete and predictable media solution for brands of all sizes. Influencer agencies can now offer their brand partners a complete media solution and media agencies can now purchase influence just like they would purchase any other piece of media. Triller's ability to guarantee views allows influencers to post across multiple platforms, and the effective CPM will be lower than any other influencer purchase to date. Brands can now shift their dollars to influencer and organic brand integrations that drive higher conversions and growth with the predictability they deserve..."

While this move, towards providing monetization options for influencers, had to be anticipated as a necessity to attract more talent and brands alike, what stands out is Triller's promise to what the service does!

"...Dubbed Crosshype, the product allows influencer marketing to be bought with guaranteed views and a calculable CPM. Never before has an app been able to guarantee views on their platform while also allowing influencers to post across multiple other platforms, transforming the way influence can be purchased and planned...."

Guaranteed views? The guaranteed CPM is however no big surprise, as the cost per mille (CPM) describes the cost per 1000 views. The downside is, of course, that CPM metrics are great for brand campaigns, but stand against the focus of marketers towards performance campaigns. Nevertheless, introducing measurability and controllability of the influencer to brand relationship is an interesting move. A move that helps marketers to overcome a century long issue, that a lot of spending on modern technology, has not yet solved. This is the issue of marketing accountability.[66] Triller's guaranteed CPM, introduces cost transparency, which will surely find great appreciation by the market. To add to this, Triller has partnered with Influential, an influencer measurement firm to help track influencer campaigns and evaluate their effectiveness.[67]

In a further move, Triller has added programmatic advertising options to its app, by partnering with advertising technology company Consumable.[68] This would enable Triller to have ad-placements in its feed; the extent and option offered are unknown. Further, this is expected to increase the reach of Triller to another 250 million users throughout the ComScore publisher network.[69] To find out more about Consumable, scan the following QR-Code.

[66] https://www.wsj.com/articles/average-tenure-of-cmos-falls-again-11590573600

[67] https://www.businessofapps.com/news/triller-partners-with-influential-on-app-influencer-marketing/

[68] https://www.mobilemarketer.com/news/triller-adds-programmatic-ads-amid-rival-tiktoks-continued-uncertainty/586368/

[69] https://www.prnewswire.com/news-releases/triller-partners-with-digital-advertising-platform-consumable-giving-triller-access-to-its-250-million-users-301144936.html

All of the above shows a clear tendency that Triller is preparing for the advertising monetization of its platform at scale.

Additionally, Triller is preparing a "Brand lab", which is aimed at helping its brand partners to create authentic content for its platform.[70] With many brands still struggling with the format of short video and how to engage Generation Z effectively, this is a very smart move.

Based on Triller's existing brand promotions, such as the Tyson comeback, or a music concert with various stars, engaging on its artistic side seems to be well perceived by brands.[71] Can Triller become the cultural hub for brands? A safe haven in the world of content-edgy short videos?

Fun fact: Triller has trademarked the term "social streaming"; is this a further hint at a potential way of differentiation from other platforms?

In summary, one could argue that Triller is taking on a more supportive role in the brand to consumer interaction than TikTok. The latter is known for its controlling nature.

For further readings, I also suggest regularly consulting the Influencer Marketing Hub on the latest marketing advice on

---

[70] https://www.roundabout.social/post/triller-video-app-is-prepping-a-content-creation-brand-lab

[71] https://www.thedrum.com/news/2020/10/21/triller-pitching-its-wares-brands-can-it-grow-tiktok-killer

the platform. To access a recent article, scan the following QR-Code.

STEP UP to the mic

Triller has already engaged with various brands. One partnership, that seems to exploit the social nature of the trademarked term "social streaming", was the "STEP UP to the Mic" talent competition, supported by boost mobile.[72] See figure 46 for more.

Figure 46. Step Up to the Mic

This competition is interesting for the fact, that it centered around music and took up the current media notion of reality-tv talent shows to Triller. It required the download and use of the Triller app to participate. The competition and setup showcased Triller's tight ties with the music industry and its true star power. Triller further differentiated its talent show

____

[72] https://www.businesswire.com/news/home/20200508005100/en/Triller-"Step-Up-to-the-Mic"-Talent-Search-Competition-to-Award-Record-Deal

from other offerings by providing the winner talent support for their first officially released song. As such, the winner will be able to perform a song featuring Quavo and Takeoff. The song itself is written by Starrah and produced by Murda Beatz. It doesn't get much better than this to reach Generation Z in an engaging and non-transactionally focused manner. This is a truly refreshing change, compared to most other platforms that feature predominantly transactionally oriented brand content.

The competition was also launched during the COVID-19 pandemic, which catapulted attention to digital forms of entertainment to new heights.[73] To learn more about the "STEP UP to the mic" talent competition and for video insights, scan the following QR-Code.

---

[73] https://www.rollingstone.com/pro/news/triller-quavo-music-singing-competition-1004327/

Safety on Triller

Like with all platforms and technology, the safe and responsible usage of Triller is much dependent on the user. Although Triller has not yet made headlines for violating users' safety or for posing a security threat, there are some aspects to look out for. These are not specific to Triller, but general aspects of user safety, particularly for minors.

Generally, Triller is available for all user aged 13 or above. For users aged 13 to 18, Triller requires the consent by parents or legal guardians to create an account. This mirrors the terms and conditions of TikTok with regards to the minimum required signup age.[74] Triller's Community Guidelines, regulating interactions on the platform, as well as its Terms of Service, can be easily access via the following QR-Codes. To the most part, these mirror the respective documents of most other platforms and do therefore not require an in-depth discussion.

---

[74] https://go.triller.co/terms/triller_terms.pdf

Community Guidelines

Scan the following QR-Code to get to Triller's community guidelines.

With regards to Triller's Community Guidelines, little is yet known about Triller's guidelines enforcement. TikTok is known for its automated Community Guidelines enforcement, which the platform also openly states in its transparency report.[75] There, TikTok claims to have removed 104'443'719 videos for violating its Community Guidelines, or 1% of its total video content. 9.4% of those videos were removed in the US and over 90% of removed videos were detected before users on the platform even saw them. To read TikTok's transparency report, scan the following QR-Code.

Triller so far announced to censor conspiracy related content, which would fall under the Community Guideline

---

[75] https://newsroom.tiktok.com/en-us/our-h-1-2020-transparency-report

enforcement,[76] yet user restrictions, or the punishment of users through temporary bans, shadow bans, or even permanent bans is yet unknown.

---

[76] https://www.insider.com/triller-announces-ban-on-qanon-conspiracy-theory-content-tiktok-tech-2020-10

Terms of Service

Scan the following QR-Code to get to Triller's terms of service.

Triller's Terms of Service should of course be read by any user signing up to the platform. In reality, only a fraction of users will ever do so.

In case you suddenly feel an irresistible urge to read these documents, you can also find them in the Triller app, under your profile, profile settings, scrolling to the bottom of the screen. See figure 47.

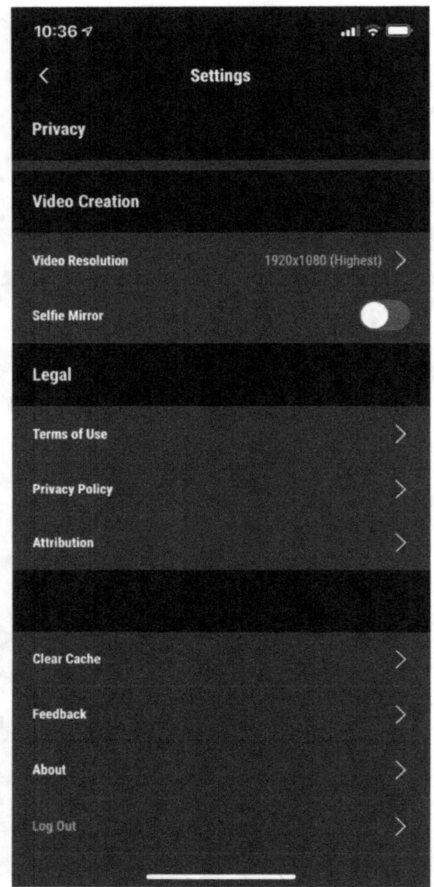

Figure 47. In-App legal documents

Privacy Policy

To view Triller's privacy policy, regulating the collecting and use of user data, please scan the following QR-Code.

Triller has greatly exploited the negativity around TikTok by assuring user privacy through a much tighter privacy policy. This was a factor, as mentioned earlier, that already drove various creators to switch in Triller's favor. A Business Insider India article even claims that Triller is only looking into the musical preferences of its users and neglects to monitor location data.[77] Reading Triller's privacy policy, Triller states the user's need to opt-in for the use of location data. See also the following extract from Triller's privacy policy (Feb 2020).

"Location Data. Information about your location when accessing and/or using the Platform, if you chose to opt-in. With your permission, we may collect Global Positioning System (GPS) data and mobile device location information. If you do not wish to share your precise location with us, you can switch off location services via the settings on your mobile device. You can also tag your location in connection with certain UGC that you create via the Platform. If you do not

---

[77] https://www.businessinsider.in/advertising/ad-tech/article/how-triller-app-smartly-poached-top-tiktokers-and-its-cso-to-become-the-no-1-in-app-store-with-zero-marketing-budget/articleshow/77614603.cms

want to share your location with others, do not tag your location in any UGC."

To contrast, TikTok's section regarding the use of location data reads as follows.

"Location data. We collect information about your location, including location information based on your SIM card and/or IP address. With your permission, we may also collect Global Positioning System (GPS) data."[78]

Both privacy policies refer to the US or global users, thus they are somewhat comparable. Refraining from starting a legal discussion, it appears that Triller's privacy policy regarding the use of location data is much more user friendly and opt-in oriented than TikTok's. In fact, TikTok's first sentence explicitly states the use of the location data.

Further, I need to detail two effects, impacting the safety of minors in particular, which are not specific to Triller, but relevant to all social media platforms, or the exposure of minors to online services.

---

[78] https://www.tiktok.com/legal/privacy-policy?lang=en#privacy-us

Predators

Minors exposing themselves online, run the danger of attracting the attention of potential predators. As said, this happens not just on Triller, but on all digital services accessible. Yet content on Triller, TikTok and Snapchat for example lends itself well to increase the attractiveness of these platforms to potential predators. Even the increasing online activity of minors, through forced online education since the start of the COVID-19 pandemic, has opened up the field for predators to prey on their victims.[79] The main target group of online predators seems to fall between the age of 11 and 15, thus towards the lower end of Triller's and other platforms' user demographic.[80] This poses a tremendous problem, if one assumes that minors are very open to share personal data online and are much less focused on issues of privacy than older generations.[81] On Snapchat, another social media platform mainly frequented by younger generations, this has already escalated into a serious problem.[82] TikTok has also already been flagged as a potential threat,[83] to which the app has responded to by allowing private profiles, restricted content sharing and a family pairing mode, which allows

---

[79] https://www.nbcnewyork.com/news/coronavirus/online-sex-predators-are-targeting-kids-during-online-learning-fbi-warns/2387079/

[80] https://www.nbcnewyork.com/news/coronavirus/online-sex-predators-are-targeting-kids-during-online-learning-fbi-warns/2387079/

[81] https://www.rga.com/futurevision/pov/gen-z-and-privacy-theyre-less-conflicted-than-other-generations

[82] https://www.wbur.org/hereandnow/2018/01/22/snapchat-child-predators

[83] https://www.familyzone.com/anz/families/blog/kids-are-obsessed-with-tiktok-so-are-predators

parents to partly monitor the activity and interaction of their kids on the app.[84]

Triller is yet missing a feature of that sort, other than the ability to set an account to private.

Thus, it is up to parents to educate their children about the safe and responsible use of any online media, which includes Triller. I highly recommend parents to consume media on social platforms, too. This helps to understand trends, user challenges and thus popular content forms. It allows to have a knowledgeable discussion with your children about the viewed content and what this content means for you or for your kids.

The FBI provides a wealth of information for parents on how to best protect kids online. You can also find contact details to report any suspicious behavior. Scan the following QR-Code to get to the relevant FBI site.

---

[84] https://newsroom.tiktok.com/en-us/tiktok-introduces-family-pairing

Cyberbullying & Peer Pressure

Another danger lurking online is that of cyberbullying. Recent US surveys indicate, that over 15% of kids fell victim to a form a cyberbullying.[85] It is thus important to understand the main differences of cyberbullying to traditional forms of bullying. Whilst this is no attempt to downplay the harm caused by traditional forms of bullying, cyberbullying amplifies this effect through its:

- persistency
- permanent nature, and
- difficulty to detect by parents or legal guardians.

One must thus not ignore the impact the 24/7 online mindset has brought along. If you fall victim to a cyberbullying attack, it is persistent in nature due to the constant availability of services and platforms involved and the very device that has changed all our lives: the smartphone. Who doesn't wake up to first check the latest gossip on Facebook, the news on Twitter, or the new follower count on Triller? The smartphone is always with us, wherever we are. Thus, cyberbullies, too. Further, the phrase "what happens in Vegas, stays in Vegas" does not apply to the online world. What happens online, stays forever. Even if platforms remove content or hate speech, their records are likely to persist somewhere else. Lastly, cyberbullying can be silent. It shows no signs of physical abuse, no noise and no alert notification. It is thus vital for parents to be sensitive to any change in notable behavior of their children and to listen to any signs of potential

---

85 https://www.stopbullying.gov/cyberbullying/what-is-it

cyberbullying to detect it early. You can hardly prevent it from happening, but your kids will need you to get through it. To show the extent of what cyberbullying can do to kids, one must only look at some prominent cases, such as the earlier mentioned Bella Poarch on TikTok, or the even more prominent case of Rebecca Black.

Rebecca Black fell victim to probably the world's most extreme case of cyberbullying. At the age of 13, in 2011, Rebecca Black released a music video on YouTube, called "Friday", see figure 48.

Figure 48. Rebecca Black Friday

To listen to her hit song, scan the following QR-Code.

As you can see in figure 48, the song went viral and shows to date almost 150 million views, but also a staggering 3.8 million dislikes. It was voted the worst song ever and its comment section literally exploded. Countless parodies of the song started to emerge, while many users published very hurtful comments; Rebecca Black even received death threats. As a result, Rebecca Black shut down, stopped going to school and finished her education in home schooling. Since we were all 13 once in our lives, we can probably imagine how that must feel! Gladly, Rebecca Black has recovered, performs music actively again and speaks openly about cyberbullying.[86] A recent blog post of hers can be accessed by scanning the following QR-Code.

For more information, practical tips, helplines and counseling, please refer to stopbullying.gov, an official site by the US government. Similar sites and portals can be found in almost

---

[86] https://www.rebeccablackonline.com

every country. These sites can be found easily by the means of a simple Google search. For the official US information site, scan the following QR-Code.

Equally important and relating to both cyberbullying, as well as to the threat of predators, is the effect of group pressure amongst teenagers to participate in challenges on platforms. As a teenager, you want to be cool, you want to belong to a group, prove your status and find yourself. This involves doing things, that you are less proud of, or think differently of when getting older. Obviously, we would have all done the same years ago, but luckily, we had no smartphone to capture our attempts to be cool. If records of our teenage years existed, we'd all surely feel very embarrassed of our behavior.

An example of one of the many trends and challenges can be found under the hashtag #wapdancechallenge. I leave it up to you to find this hashtag and decide for yourself, if you want to see your kids replicating that choreography or use the soundtrack for that matter.

Just in case: I'm not prude and find the WAP a rather catchy tune. I am however 41 years old and assume to have a very low risk of becoming the victim of an online predator. Thus, even if all my friends would do the #wapdancechallenge, my biggest threat in joining in would be to publicly embarrass myself, or to jeopardize a future job opportunity.

Thus, parents need to educate their kids about the dangers and effects their online behavior can cause today, but also in the future. As said, what happens online, stays forever!

Influencer effects

Let's get to the true ugly. The reason your kids want now product A over product B. Influencers! Influencers are the weed growing on the increasing Ad-Blocker usage. Roughly 30% of Internet users enable a form of Ad-Blocking technology.[87] Thus, the already declining advertising effectiveness continues to further deteriorate. The escape vehicle of brands are influencers. These are building on the principles of word of mouth and step in to bridge the advertising-gap from brands to consumers. So far, so good. The evolution of advertising has been an endless rat race, an infinite cat and mouse game and the fundament of most digital business models. We get to this in the next section in more detail.

So, what is the influencer effect? The influencer effect, in my opinion, is the reality distortion of young users leading to the misinterpretation of the true intentions of most influencers. In other words, most teenagers miss to recognize the transactional or monetization motive of today's influencers. This makes them particularly prone to falling for advertised products or services by their much-admired influencer.

---

[87] https://www.emarketer.com/content/ad-blocking-growth-is-slowing-down-but-not-going-away

Figure 49. A want to be influencer's true intentions

Research studies have shown, that kids below the age of 12 are prone to misjudge the influencer – follower relationship as a form of friendship. Influencers start to take on the roles of friends and idols. This serves the process of identifying yourself, developing your own identity, while having a group to belong to. Whilst this might sound OK in theory, it holds tremendous danger if this feeling of identity, friendship and idolism is only met by one side of the relationship equation.

I highly recommend parents to talk to their children, helping them identify and understand the true intentions of influencers in their life. This could start by looking at the very definition of the word influencer. The Oxford Learner's Dictionaries defines the term influencer as follows. Please refer to figure 50.

Figure 50. Influencer definition

This definition, although still diplomatic, highlights the ability and intend to influence, that alter a decision-making behavior or actions, towards a disclosed or promoted product. Btw. did you know that influencers' suggestions have almost the same impact as those of friends and family? Some research suggests, the difference is in the single percentage points, thus making influencers even more prone to impact purchasing decision making processes by exhibiting their seemingly perfect, ever happy, successful and fun-filled lives.

An enabling factor for the above is of course the low, or even missing, advertising literacy of teenagers and young kids. Depending on the age group, children have not yet developed advertising literacy.[88] This refers to the ability to recognize advertising attempts and to understand that these attempts are being made to advocate the purchase of a product or service. This holds true with all forms of advertising, yet the earlier described reality distortion, with regards to the assumed influencer relationship, propels this effect to higher levels.

---

[88] https://news.illinois.edu/view/6367/321624

Chapter 4: Persuasive Technologies

In 2020 and following, there should be no book about any technology platform without a chapter, or at the very minimum some pages about persuasive technologies. At least since the release of Netflix's documentary "the Social Dilemma", does the world know about the existence of persuasive technologies. If you have not yet watched "the Social Dilemma", I highly recommend you do so! Scan the following QR-Code to get to homepage of "the Social Dilemma".

But why do I think you should watch this documentary? Do I believe in conspiracies? Or that COVID-19 is a hoax? No! Not really! But every piece of digital technology you use, is impacting your life, your behavior and maybe even your opinions and attitudes. This is the true danger of digitalization! This is the danger of modern society! And it is the danger of a raging conflict of interest between privacy rights, advertisers, politics and platforms. The user and content creators are stuck in the middle! They have become the product of the digital world!

I know! It sounds like a conspiracy theory! I have been talking about this for years and truly believe, that everybody using a smartphone, creating a profile on an app, or a platform, or even running a Google search, should at least be informed about what is happening.

Thus, let's go!

So, what are these mysterious persuasive technologies? Persuasive technologies are technologies, which hold the power to influence, impact or alter a user's behavior. Examples for this include the notification function of your smartphone's operating system (OS). Whilst notifications might have been designed to notify you of any new information, such as an E-Mail or a message, they have been proven to draw users back into an app.

Technology companies, such as Triller, Google, Facebook, TikTok and pretty much every other app, or platform make use of these persuasive technologies. But why? To increase time spent in-app or on-platform and user engagement! But why? Ok! Are you ready for this? To generate advertising opportunities. The more time a user spends on a platform and the higher the user's engagement, the more profitable it is to serve this user advertising. The more interesting it becomes for brands to buy advertising on the platform. The user thus becomes the actual product! Yep, you heard that right! Have you ever wondered why it is free to use Facebook, Triller, TikTok, Instagram or YouTube? After all, these platforms spend insane amounts on development, maintenance and storage, to let you share every second of your life with the world. Why is it that you have to pay for the use of Dropbox to store your vacation pictures, but not if you do so on Facebook? Because you are the actual product!

Through the sharing of your personal data, your online behavior, your every click and use of technology, you are being monitored and classified by algorithms. Facebook uses 52'000 attributes to classify users! I guess you are shocked now! I recommend reading this ProPublica article by scanning the following QR-Code.

But wait, it gets worse! We have now established, that platforms monitor your online behavior, track your journey and enrich their data with third party data, acquired via data brokerage firms. They use this data to let advertisers target you, thus your data is the enabler and your time the key to have a running money-making advertising platform. But there is one more problem! You cannot engage a user just by using persuasive technologies, no matter how persuasive they are. The next piece you need to master is the content. Most platforms do not create their own content. They function merely as a transactional space to match content creators to user interests and brands' advertising to user interests. This is where powerful algorithms come to the scene.

Before we however continue, let's have a look at figure 51 for an overview of platform dynamics.

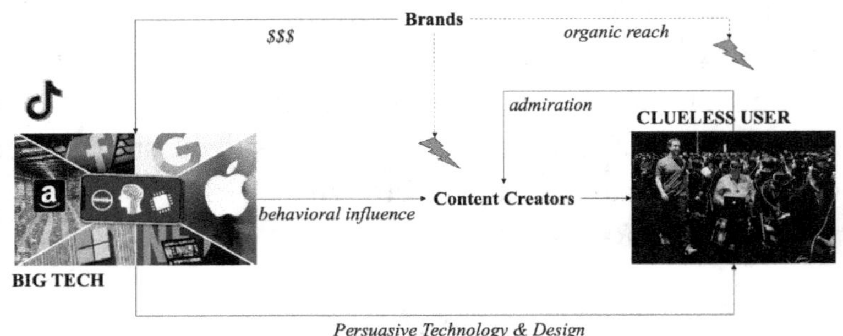

Figure 51. Platform dynamics

Thus, platforms need to entice content creators to create engaging and monetizable content. Further, they need to engage users to come to the platform and stay as long as possible. Finally, they need to get their money-making machine going. How? By restricting brand's organic reach on the platform. Did you know that Facebook's average organic reach for non-sponsored brand content is around 5% and decreasing?

One to control them all!

Platform's, particularly mega platforms, have thus the ability to control and influence all relevant aspects impacting their own objective: monetization. Can it get any better? I hardly think so.

Just look at Facebook's earnings results in a year, in which most businesses struggled to stay afloat. In a year when the world was struck by a global pandemic, Facebook's advertising revenue grew by 10%. It's net income by 98%.

In millions, except percentages and per share amounts	Three Months Ended June 30,		Year-over-Year %
	2020	2019 [1]	Change
Revenue:			
Advertising	$ 18,321	$ 16,624	10%
Other	366	262	40%
Total revenue	18,687	16,886	11%
Total costs and expenses	12,724	12,260	4%
Income from operations	$ 5,963	$ 4,626	29%
Operating margin	32%	27%	
Provision for income taxes	$ 953	$ 2,216	(57)%
Effective tax rate	16%	46%	
Net income	$ 5,178	$ 2,616	98%
Diluted earnings per share (EPS)	$ 1.80	$ 0.91	98%

Figure 52. Facebook's Q2 2020 results[89]

It has to be noted, that 2019 included a USD 2 billion legal expense and a USD 1.1 billion tax expense. Still, 10% advertising growth is remarkable, while the global economy is projected to grow a negative 5% in 2020.[90]

Let's take this up a notch. If we assume that technology companies have the ability to influence their bottom line by orchestrating all players involved, through either algorithms or platform mechanics, why does nobody interfere? Why does nobody say: STOP! Enough is enough!

For this, let's look at who this somebody could be! Brands? Well, their main goal is to reach consumers and their focus has very much shifted to advertising, more advertising, advertising on top of advertising and advertising. Advertising equals turnover and the fear to lose advertising opportunities exceeds most brands' ability to identify alternate scenarios. Also, most

---

[89] https://investor.fb.com/investor-news/press-release-details/2020/Facebook-Reports-Second-Quarter-2020-Results/default.aspx

[90] https://www.imf.org/en/Publications/WEO/Issues/2020/06/24/WEOUpdateJune2020

brands lack truly innovative products to WOW the market without the need to constantly push their messages in the face of their consumers. Exceptions apply, such as Tesla, which is known for its USD 0 advertising budget. As I have put it in an article, advertising is the cost of lacking innovation. So, it is fair to say that we can rule out brands.

Let's look at users! Sure, we are fed up by advertising. But we also got used to it. Do you remember ad-free YouTube? That is really long ago. What happens now when you want to watch any content on YouTube? You are eagle-eye trained to wait for the Pre-Roll ad to finally showcase the "skip ad" button. You click that button faster than any First-Person Shooter (FPS) world champion. We call this: advertising blindness. Plus, all your friends hang out on these platforms. Maybe also your crush. So, you have no choice but to deal with it.

What about content creators? Well, since many content creators strive to become influencers and that means to create sponsored content, we can already stop the discussion here.

The platform itself is hardly going to strive for privacy or persuasion regulation. So, who else?

Oh yes. Politics! Sure, shouldn't the government and thus politics have an interest in this? After all, persuasive technologies hold the power to influence decision making and behavior, thus possible effects are far reaching. The 2016 US presidential election serves as an example. Facebook was long accused of having polarized opinions through its algorithm. Probably not actively, but through its algorithm's objective to increase engagement.[91] There is ample of research suggesting that polarizing content leads to higher user engagement, thus this is what the algorithm inevitably exploits. It has also been shown and widely discussed, that Russian accounts tried to influence the 2016 US presidential election by placing politically induced ads.[92] The Times reports advertising purchases in the height of USD 100'000 by foreign entities.[93] If you are interested in the persuasive power of Facebook and its countermeasures to avoid any political interference, I highly recommend listening to the Prof G Podcast, episode "Algorithms and the Treats to Democracy". In this episode, NYU-Stern Professor Scott Galloway interviews Yaël Eisenstat, a visiting fellow at Cornell Tech's Digital Life Initiative and former Elections Integrity Head for Political Ads at Facebook. Scan the QR-Code below to listen to the podcast.

Sounds like, politics should be interested, right? Well, here is the thing! Politicians act just like brands online. Yet instead of selling products, their goal is to get votes. This goal is equally important to entice politicians to make use of advertising opportunities online to narrowly target undecisive voters, or

[91] https://www.theatlantic.com/technology/archive/2017/10/what-facebook-did/542502/

[92] https://www.npr.org/2017/09/08/549284183/facebook-acknowledges-russian-ads-in-2016-election-will-investigations-follow?t=1605017600000

[93] https://time.com/4930532/facebook-russian-accounts-2016-election/

even opposite voters. To completely blow your mind, let's look at the advertising spending of the Trump and Biden campaign in the 2020 US presidential elections. Facebook discloses political advertising spending in its Ad Library, which is accessible to everybody. Doing so doesn't even require a Facebook account. To access Facebook's Ad Library, scan the following QR-Code.

Ok, now let's look into the spending of both Trump and Biden. You better sit down for that. The numbers you will be shown are Facebook placement spending only. That means third party costs and the cost of creation are excluded. Also, to highlight it again, it is only spending on Facebook. Let's start with Trump, see figure 53.

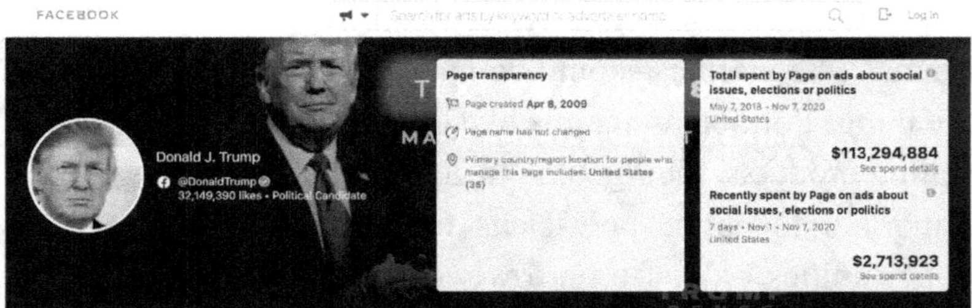

Figure 53. Trump's Facebook spending

Not bad, USD 113 million since May 2018, thus mid-term and the beginning of the 2020 campaigning efforts. At the time of writing this book, on the 10th November 2020, there were no more active ads running. In other words, the interest in votes and thus the interest to reach the populations has ceased. The newly elected president of the US, Joe Biden, shows the following numbers. See figure 54.

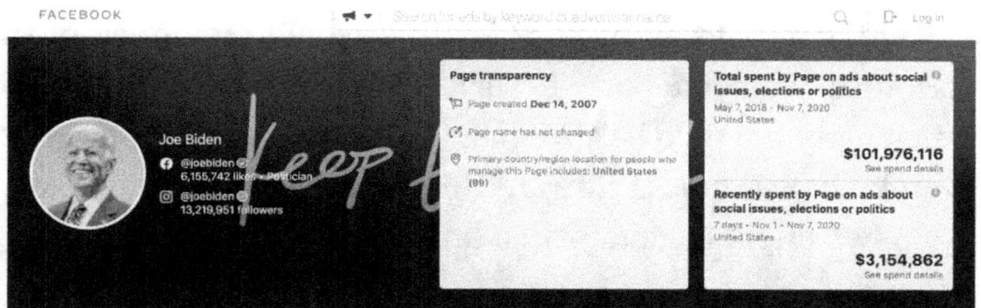

Figure 54. Biden's Facebook spending

Similarly, to Trump, Biden stopped all ads on the 3rd of November. Now ad on top both vice presidents, relevant parties and supporters and you end up with a Facebook advertising spending of around USD 250 to 300 million for the 2020 US presidential election.

Thus, we see that the hidden, or maybe not so hidden agenda of politicians make also use of your data. Therefore, do not expect politicians to ever speak up against the persuasive power of technology.

Is all hope lost? Well, no! Consumers do actually have a certain choice. You have a choice to disable notifications in your phone's settings to reduce the impact these luring tactics have on your daily life. You can think about your active decision making and which content you truly aim to consume, vs. which content you are being served by an algorithm. The same applies of course to your purchasing decision making processes. Just try to be aware of influencing factors and you regain control, at least partly. The rat race will however continue; technology will become savvier to read us and algorithms more relentless.

Is there an end to all of this? Well, it would require an open discourse and some party to manage that discourse. But who is that party going to be? We have so far pretty much ruled out everybody and unless Edward Snowden steps up to the plate again, we might have to wait a little longer.

However, another alternative is to discuss the value of privacy. How much is your very privacy worth to you, and would you pay to regain your privacy, or be willing to give it up at a cost. This question has been explored in recent studies, with surprising results. To read a scientific study on the topic, scan the following QR-Code.

Another study, which is less scientific in nature, compared the revenue of selected social platforms per user with the amount people would be willing to pay for a privacy protecting experience. You will be surprised to learn, that Facebook could for instance increase its revenue by protecting users'

privacy. However, this very study, see figure 55, is based on a sample size of only 1000 users, thus hardly representable.

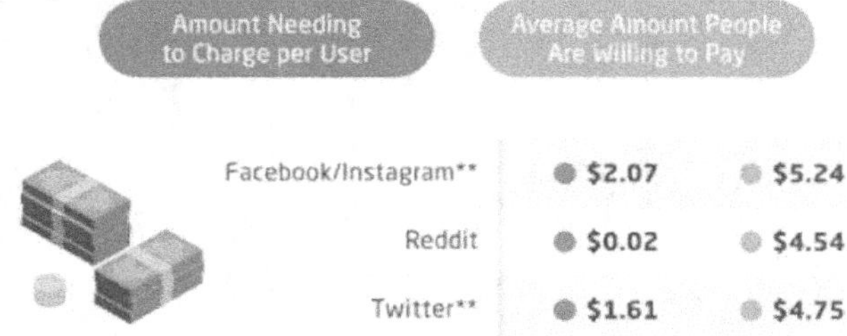

Figure 55. Non-Ad supported platform revenue

If you want to however try an ad-free, privacy protecting alternative to Facebook, MeWe is your best bet. Please let me know how that goes for you.[94]

It is important to note, that I am not suggesting that Triller is on the same trajectory as all other platforms and apps, to make you the product. However, as note earlier: history has a tendency to repeat itself.

Thus, let's see what happens!

---

[94] https://mewe.com

Is Triller a true TikTok alternative?

This book was meant to be about 25-30 pages long, a booklet about Triller as the potential rising star in the short video circuit. As life has it, it became slightly longer, slightly broader and probably slightly more polarizing. But is Triller a true alternative to TikTok, or just another copycat, a replacement in the face of a looming TikTok ban?

Well! Personally, I will continue my journey on TikTok for now. There are a few things I still need to explore, understand and experiment with. A few studies to conduct and a few papers to write. Equally however, I will intensify my journey on Triller. From what Triller has shown so far, it holds the potential to stand up against TikTok. It's deep integration into the music world and its innovative focus on social streaming, poise Triller to capture market share in various age groups. Triller's move to make itself appealing to influencers[95] helps to attract younger and short video savvy audiences quickly to the app.

At the same time, I believe that Triller needs to find a clear position; not as a TikTok replacement, in the event of a TikTok-ban, but as a true standalone alternative. Triller seems to have the tools, the team and network to pull this off.

Thus, get on the app now! Secure your account and profile!

---

[95] https://www.accesswire.com/609622/Admist-Looming-TikTok-Ban-Triller-Offers-Influencers-Three-Times-More-Than-TikTok-On-New-Go-Live-Feature

Remember, the early bird…

About the author

Whom am I? On Triller and TikTok, I am the @marketing_guy. In the real world, I am also known as Markus Rach. I am currently a lecturer at the University of Applied Sciences and Arts Northwestern Switzerland. I teach marketing, digital marketing, sales and technology related subjects. I also teach at the Swiss Marketing Academy and am a guest lecturer at the Shenzhen Technology University in China.

As a hobby, I work on my DBA, assessing the impact of Marketing Technologies on the Marketing Return on Investment. I also serve as an advisory board member to the CMO Council and run a boutique marketing consultancy. Before experimenting in academia, I managed and restructured marketing departments for multinational B2Bs. I remain a marketer at heart!

More importantly, I have two kids, Maximilian and Sophie, who see far too little of me. Love you guys, to the moon and back! I also have the most supportive rockstar wife, a crazy marketer could ever dream of. My high school sweetheart and probably the only person who's able to deal with my constant flux of ideas: Jeanette. Love you!

I cannot end it here though. My family would not be complete without the mention of our two fluffy companions: Xita our Cavalier King Charles Spaniel and Sammy, the bomber,

Golden Retriever. Before you even wonder: YES, they do have their own social media accounts!

Let's rock!

Figure 56. Me and my wonderful family

One more thing!

Yes, I stole that line from Apple! Shame on me!

But I do also have one more thing! I would sincerely appreciate your feedback. Either as a reference on Amazon, as an E-Mail, or as a LinkedIn comment.

I sincerely enjoyed working on this little book and hope you found it insightful!

Thank you!

Markus Rach
markusrach@hotmail.com

www.ingramcontent.com/pod-product-compliance
Lightning Source LLC
Chambersburg PA
CBHW061353250726
48657CB00004B/1476